CHINA'S
HEILONGJIANG PROVINCE
PART 5

黑龙江省

MENGMENG FU
付萌萌

PREFACE

Let's learn Chinese characters, words, phrases, and simple sentences with Chinese names, surnames and geography (中国地理). Each book contains numerous geographic details of Chinese administrative divisions (city, county, provinces). The characters are presented with English and pinyin.

CONTENTS

CHAPTER 1: NAMES & LOCATIONS (1-30)

601。姓名: 乔豪秀

住址（家庭）：黑龙江省双鸭山市友谊县愈斌路 246 号波游公寓 38 层 265 室（邮政编码：224310）。联系电话：42536276。电子邮箱：srngm@fmetuydj.cn

Zhù zhǐ: Qiáo Háo Xiù Hēilóngjiāng Shěng Shuāngyāshān Shì Yǒuyì Xiàn Yù Bīn Lù 246 Hào Bō Yóu Gōng Yù 38 Céng 265 Shì (Yóuzhèng Biānmǎ：224310). Liánxì Diànhuà：42536276. Diànzǐ Yóuxiāng：srngm@fmetuydj.cn

Hao Xiu Qiao, Room# 265, Floor# 38, Bo You Apartment, 246 Yu Bin Road, Youyi County, Shuangyashan, Heilongjiang. Postal Code: 224310. Phone Number：42536276. E-mail：srngm@fmetuydj.cn

602。姓名: 宗政澜源

住址（广场）：黑龙江省双鸭山市饶河县独人路 173 号阳亮广场（邮政编码：917105）。联系电话：57010076。电子邮箱：qubkf@rkgnofqv.squares.cn

Zhù zhǐ: Zōngzhèng Lán Yuán Hēilóngjiāng Shěng Shuāngyāshān Shì Ráo Hé Xiàn Dú Rén Lù 173 Hào Yáng Liàng Guǎng Chǎng (Yóuzhèng Biānmǎ：917105). Liánxì Diànhuà：57010076. Diànzǐ Yóuxiāng：qubkf@rkgnofqv.squares.cn

Lan Yuan Zongzheng, Yang Liang Square, 173 Du Ren Road, Raohe County, Shuangyashan, Heilongjiang. Postal Code: 917105. Phone Number：57010076. E-mail：qubkf@rkgnofqv.squares.cn

603。姓名: 封伦铁

住址（湖泊）：黑龙江省双鸭山市饶河县陶铁路 127 号兵谢湖（邮政编码：344252）。联系电话：87201080。电子邮箱：qdljk@peckhidz.lakes.cn

Zhù zhǐ: Fēng Lún Tiě Hēilóngjiāng Shěng Shuāngyāshān Shì Ráo Hé Xiàn Táo Fū Lù 127 Hào Bīng Xiè Hú (Yóuzhèng Biānmǎ：344252). Liánxì Diànhuà：87201080. Diànzǐ Yóuxiāng：qdljk@peckhidz.lakes.cn

Lun Tie Feng, Bing Xie Lake, 127 Tao Fu Road, Raohe County, Shuangyashan, Heilongjiang. Postal Code: 344252. Phone Number：87201080. E-mail：qdljk@peckhidz.lakes.cn

604。姓名: 阎岐俊

住址（寺庙）：黑龙江省佳木斯市汤原县独发路 868 号水跃寺（邮政编码：774935）。联系电话：12760944。电子邮箱：zbaoh@ntsjfdco.god.cn

Zhù zhǐ: Yán Qí Jùn Hēilóngjiāng Shěng Jiāmùsī Shì Tāng Yuán Xiàn Dú Fā Lù 868 Hào Shuǐ Yuè Sì (Yóuzhèng Biānmǎ：774935). Liánxì Diànhuà：12760944. Diànzǐ Yóuxiāng：zbaoh@ntsjfdco.god.cn

Qi Jun Yan, Shui Yue Temple, 868 Du Fa Road, Tangyuan County, Jiamusi, Heilongjiang. Postal Code: 774935. Phone Number：12760944. E-mail：zbaoh@ntsjfdco.god.cn

605。姓名: 酆光咚

住址（公司）：黑龙江省哈尔滨市五常市征维路 859 号陆桥有限公司（邮政编码：359495）。联系电话：20599268。电子邮箱：uxlmk@qypdulxe.biz.cn

Zhù zhǐ: Fēng Guāng Dōng Hēilóngjiāng Shěng Hāěrbīn Shì Wǔcháng Shì Zhēng Wéi Lù 859 Hào Liù Qiáo Yǒuxiàn Gōngsī (Yóuzhèng Biānmǎ：359495). Liánxì Diànhuà：20599268. Diànzǐ Yóuxiāng：uxlmk@qypdulxe.biz.cn

Guang Dong Feng, Liu Qiao Corporation, 859 Zheng Wei Road, Wuchang City, Harbin, Heilongjiang. Postal Code: 359495. Phone Number：20599268. E-mail：uxlmk@qypdulxe.biz.cn

606。姓名: 陶磊亮

住址（机场）：黑龙江省大庆市肇州县辉食路 998 号大庆队翰国际机场（邮政编码：803839）。联系电话：79389073。电子邮箱：tbvwc@gxdypknt.airports.cn

Zhù zhǐ: Táo Lěi Liàng Hēilóngjiāng Shěng Dàqìng Shì Zhào Zhōu Xiàn Huī Sì Lù 998 Hào Dàqng Duì Hàn Guó Jì Jī Chǎng (Yóuzhèng Biānmǎ：803839). Liánxì Diànhuà：79389073. Diànzǐ Yóuxiāng：tbvwc@gxdypknt.airports.cn

Lei Liang Tao, Daqing Dui Han International Airport, 998 Hui Si Road, Zhaozhou County, Daqing, Heilongjiang. Postal Code: 803839. Phone Number：79389073. E-mail：tbvwc@gxdypknt.airports.cn

607。姓名: 倪智葛

住址（寺庙）：黑龙江省双鸭山市四方台区珏敬路 231 号辙独寺（邮政编码：225488）。联系电话：61017396。电子邮箱：hzjao@doqiazlj.god.cn

Zhù zhǐ: Ní Zhì Gé Hēilóngjiāng Shěng Shuāngyāshān Shì Sìfāng Tái Qū Jué Jìng Lù 231 Hào Zhé Dú Sì（Yóuzhèng Biānmǎ：225488). Liánxì Diànhuà：61017396. Diànzǐ Yóuxiāng：hzjao@doqiazlj.god.cn

Zhi Ge Ni, Zhe Du Temple, 231 Jue Jing Road, Sifangtai District, Shuangyashan, Heilongjiang. Postal Code: 225488. Phone Number：61017396. E-mail：hzjao@doqiazlj.god.cn

608。姓名: 隆石全

住址（家庭）：黑龙江省大庆市大同区继盛路 582 号轶院公寓 40 层 749 室（邮政编码：277028）。联系电话：16479433。电子邮箱：dxbkg@stfximac.cn

Zhù zhǐ: Lóng Dàn Quán Hēilóngjiāng Shěng Dàqìng Shì Dàtóng Qū Jì Shèng Lù 582 Hào Yì Yuàn Gōng Yù 40 Céng 749 Shì（Yóuzhèng Biānmǎ：277028). Liánxì Diànhuà：16479433. Diànzǐ Yóuxiāng：dxbkg@stfximac.cn

Dan Quan Long, Room# 749, Floor# 40, Yi Yuan Apartment, 582 Ji Sheng Road, Datong District, Daqing, Heilongjiang. Postal Code: 277028. Phone Number：16479433. E-mail：dxbkg@stfximac.cn

609。姓名: 糜咚金

住址（博物院）：黑龙江省鹤岗市东山区龙恩路 376 号鹤岗博物馆（邮政编码：766984）。联系电话：61576309。电子邮箱：oqftc@brimvglo.museums.cn

Zhù zhǐ: Mí Dōng Jīn Hēilóngjiāng Shěng Hè Gǎng Shì Dōng Shānqū Lóng Ēn Lù 376 Hào Hè Gǎng Bó Wù Guǎn（Yóuzhèng Biānmǎ：766984). Liánxì Diànhuà：61576309. Diànzǐ Yóuxiāng：oqftc@brimvglo.museums.cn

Dong Jin Mi, Hegang Museum, 376 Long En Road, Dongshan District, Hegang, Heilongjiang. Postal Code: 766984. Phone Number：61576309. E-mail：oqftc@brimvglo.museums.cn

610。姓名: 韶亮亮

住址（大学）：黑龙江省鸡西市虎林市澜涛大学黎沛路 594 号（邮政编码：955112）。联系电话：66676179。电子邮箱：gmvan@zncmehrw.edu.cn

Zhù zhǐ: Sháo Liàng Liàng Hēilóngjiāng Shěng Jīxī Shì Hǔ Lín Shì Lán Tāo DàxuéLí Bèi Lù 594 Hào（Yóuzhèng Biānmǎ：955112). Liánxì Diànhuà：66676179. Diànzǐ Yóuxiāng：gmvan@zncmehrw.edu.cn

Liang Liang Shao, Lan Tao University, 594 Li Bei Road, Hulin City, Jixi, Heilongjiang. Postal Code: 955112. Phone Number：66676179. E-mail：gmvan@zncmehrw.edu.cn

611。姓名: 姓绅大

住址（公共汽车站）：黑龙江省牡丹江市爱民区葆桥路 153 号兵风站（邮政编码：183625）。联系电话：67398771。电子邮箱：uxyhf@zqdcoksa.transport.cn

Zhù zhǐ: Xìng Shēn Dài Hēilóngjiāng Shěng Mǔdānjiāng Shì Àimín Qū Bǎo Qiáo Lù 153 Hào Bīng Fēng Zhàn（Yóuzhèng Biānmǎ：183625). Liánxì Diànhuà：67398771. Diànzǐ Yóuxiāng：uxyhf@zqdcoksa.transport.cn

Shen Dai Xing, Bing Feng Bus Station, 153 Bao Qiao Road, Aimin District, Mudanjiang, Heilongjiang. Postal Code: 183625. Phone Number：67398771. E-mail：uxyhf@zqdcoksa.transport.cn

612。姓名: 梅风葆

住址（机场）：黑龙江省大兴安岭地区呼玛县宝顺路 798 号大兴安岭地区水陆国际机场（邮政编码：657650）。联系电话：98965656。电子邮箱：cvflx@rnawpjzf.airports.cn

Zhù zhǐ: Méi Fēng Bǎo Hēilóngjiāng Shěng Dàxīngānlǐng Dìqū Hū Mǎ Xiàn Bǎo Shùn Lù 798 Hào Dàxīngānlǐng Dqū Shuǐ Liù Guó Jì Jī Chǎng（Yóuzhèng Biānmǎ：657650). Liánxì Diànhuà：98965656. Diànzǐ Yóuxiāng：cvflx@rnawpjzf.airports.cn

Feng Bao Mei, Da Hinggan Ling Shui Liu International Airport, 798 Bao Shun Road, Huma County, Da Hinggan Ling, Heilongjiang. Postal Code: 657650. Phone Number：98965656. E-mail：cvflx@rnawpjzf.airports.cn

613。姓名: 左翰超

住址（博物院）：黑龙江省牡丹江市穆棱市独居路 823 号牡丹江博物馆（邮政编码：244114）。联系电话：44018178。电子邮箱：wnubq@cavkfgyi.museums.cn

Zhù zhǐ: Zuǒ Hàn Chāo Hēilóngjiāng Shěng Mǔdānjiāng Shì Mù Léng Shì Dú Jū Lù 823 Hào Mǔdānjiāng Bó Wù Guǎn (Yóuzhèng Biānmǎ：244114). Liánxì Diànhuà：44018178. Diànzǐ Yóuxiāng：wnubq@cavkfgyi.museums.cn

Han Chao Zuo, Mudanjiang Museum, 823 Du Ju Road, Mulen, Mudanjiang, Heilongjiang. Postal Code: 244114. Phone Number：44018178. E-mail：wnubq@cavkfgyi.museums.cn

614。姓名: 卫淹智

住址（医院）：黑龙江省齐齐哈尔市泰来县咚九路 989 号食盛医院（邮政编码：954136）。联系电话：40863576。电子邮箱：fghuv@dlrwqoie.health.cn

Zhù zhǐ: Wèi Yān Zhì Hēilóngjiāng Shěng Qíqíhāěr Shì Tài Lái Xiàn Dōng Jiǔ Lù 989 Hào Yì Chéng Yī Yuàn (Yóuzhèng Biānmǎ：954136). Liánxì Diànhuà：40863576. Diànzǐ Yóuxiāng：fghuv@dlrwqoie.health.cn

Yan Zhi Wei, Yi Cheng Hospital, 989 Dong Jiu Road, Tailai County, Qiqihar, Heilongjiang. Postal Code: 954136. Phone Number：40863576. E-mail：fghuv@dlrwqoie.health.cn

615。姓名: 俞宽陆

住址（公共汽车站）：黑龙江省绥化市海伦市铭大路 984 号己禹站（邮政编码：972564）。联系电话：27221093。电子邮箱：yplxg@knbltxdu.transport.cn

Zhù zhǐ: Yú Kuān Liù Hēilóngjiāng Shěng Suíhuà Shì Hǎilún Shì Míng Dà Lù 984 Hào Jǐ Yǔ Zhàn (Yóuzhèng Biānmǎ：972564). Liánxì Diànhuà：27221093. Diànzǐ Yóuxiāng：yplxg@knbltxdu.transport.cn

Kuan Liu Yu, Ji Yu Bus Station, 984 Ming Da Road, Helen, Suihua, Heilongjiang. Postal Code: 972564. Phone Number：27221093. E-mail：yplxg@knbltxdu.transport.cn

616。姓名: 颜祥石

住址（酒店）：黑龙江省牡丹江市西安区土歧路 958 号翰黎酒店（邮政编码：195130）。联系电话：79818307。电子邮箱：zpofr@barvhmcx.biz.cn

Zhù zhǐ: Yán Xiáng Dàn Hēilóngjiāng Shěng Mǔdānjiāng Shì Xīān Qū Tǔ Qí Lù 958 Hào Hàn Lí Jiǔ Diàn（Yóuzhèng Biānmǎ：195130). Liánxì Diànhuà：79818307. Diànzǐ Yóuxiāng：zpofr@barvhmcx.biz.cn

Xiang Dan Yan, Han Li Hotel, 958 Tu Qi Road, Xian District, Mudanjiang, Heilongjiang. Postal Code: 195130. Phone Number：79818307. E-mail：zpofr@barvhmcx.biz.cn

617。姓名: 商不舟

住址（医院）：黑龙江省鸡西市鸡冠区山人路 467 号强坚医院（邮政编码：795548）。联系电话：14688904。电子邮箱：qlspz@rexwkdya.health.cn

Zhù zhǐ: Shāng Bù Zhōu Hēilóngjiāng Shěng Jīxī Shì Jīguān Qū Shān Rén Lù 467 Hào Qiáng Jiān Yī Yuàn（Yóuzhèng Biānmǎ：795548). Liánxì Diànhuà：14688904. Diànzǐ Yóuxiāng：qlspz@rexwkdya.health.cn

Bu Zhou Shang, Qiang Jian Hospital, 467 Shan Ren Road, Cockscomb District, Jixi, Heilongjiang. Postal Code: 795548. Phone Number：14688904. E-mail：qlspz@rexwkdya.health.cn

618。姓名: 戚成南

住址（博物院）：黑龙江省大庆市肇源县翼珏路 620 号大庆博物馆（邮政编码：787576）。联系电话：46221816。电子邮箱：kwcdx@oqzmfhkc.museums.cn

Zhù zhǐ: Qī Chéng Nán Hēilóngjiāng Shěng Dàqìng Shì Zhào Yuán Xiàn Yì Jué Lù 620 Hào Dàqng Bó Wù Guǎn（Yóuzhèng Biānmǎ：787576). Liánxì Diànhuà：46221816. Diànzǐ Yóuxiāng：kwcdx@oqzmfhkc.museums.cn

Cheng Nan Qi, Daqing Museum, 620 Yi Jue Road, Zhaoyuan County, Daqing, Heilongjiang. Postal Code: 787576. Phone Number：46221816. E-mail：kwcdx@oqzmfhkc.museums.cn

619。姓名: 红宝友

住址（大学）：黑龙江省大庆市杜尔伯特蒙古族自治县龙己大学甫鸣路 135 号（邮政编码：321139）。联系电话：86287252。电子邮箱：grdmv@vuhczfdx.edu.cn

Zhù zhǐ: Hóng Bǎo Yǒu Hēilóngjiāng Shěng Dàqìng Shì Dù Ěr Bó Tè Ménggǔ Zú Zìzhìxiàn Lóng Jǐ DàxuéFǔ Míng Lù 135 Hào (Yóuzhèng Biānmǎ：321139). Liánxì Diànhuà：86287252. Diànzǐ Yóuxiāng：grdmv@vuhczfdx.edu.cn

Bao You Hong, Long Ji University, 135 Fu Ming Road, Duerbot Mongolian Autonomous County, Daqing, Heilongjiang. Postal Code: 321139. Phone Number：86287252. E-mail：grdmv@vuhczfdx.edu.cn

620。姓名: 公良鹤仲

住址（公园）：黑龙江省大庆市肇源县大黎路 292 号石歧公园（邮政编码：404714）。联系电话：66839419。电子邮箱：sgiqw@nqgvowhy.parks.cn

Zhù zhǐ: Gōngliáng Hè Zhòng Hēilóngjiāng Shěng Dàqìng Shì Zhào Yuán Xiàn Dài Lí Lù 292 Hào Dàn Qí Gōng Yuán (Yóuzhèng Biānmǎ：404714). Liánxì Diànhuà：66839419. Diànzǐ Yóuxiāng：sgiqw@nqgvowhy.parks.cn

He Zhong Gongliang, Dan Qi Park, 292 Dai Li Road, Zhaoyuan County, Daqing, Heilongjiang. Postal Code: 404714. Phone Number：66839419. E-mail：sgiqw@nqgvowhy.parks.cn

621。姓名: 田辉陶

住址（博物院）：黑龙江省大庆市林甸县领员路 187 号大庆博物馆（邮政编码：570015）。联系电话：86330878。电子邮箱：phoyi@bjrfanto.museums.cn

Zhù zhǐ: Tián Huī Táo Hēilóngjiāng Shěng Dàqìng Shì Lín Diānxiàn Lǐng Yún Lù 187 Hào Dàqng Bó Wù Guǎn (Yóuzhèng Biānmǎ: 570015). Liánxì Diànhuà: 86330878. Diànzǐ Yóuxiāng: phoyi@bjrfanto.museums.cn

Hui Tao Tian, Daqing Museum, 187 Ling Yun Road, Lindian County, Daqing, Heilongjiang. Postal Code: 570015. Phone Number: 86330878. E-mail: phoyi@bjrfanto.museums.cn

622。姓名: 魏柱刚

住址（公园）：黑龙江省牡丹江市宁安市振启路 426 号维威公园（邮政编码：446637）。联系电话：63334274。电子邮箱：khtnr@jpfdbvos.parks.cn

Zhù zhǐ: Wèi Zhù Gāng Hēilóngjiāng Shěng Mǔdānjiāng Shì Níng Ān Shì Zhèn Qǐ Lù 426 Hào Wéi Wēi Gōng Yuán (Yóuzhèng Biānmǎ: 446637). Liánxì Diànhuà: 63334274. Diànzǐ Yóuxiāng: khtnr@jpfdbvos.parks.cn

Zhu Gang Wei, Wei Wei Park, 426 Zhen Qi Road, Ningan, Mudanjiang, Heilongjiang. Postal Code: 446637. Phone Number: 63334274. E-mail: khtnr@jpfdbvos.parks.cn

623。姓名: 单黎鹤

住址（公司）：黑龙江省鹤岗市兴安区熔亭路 962 号启焯有限公司（邮政编码：541402）。联系电话：84588533。电子邮箱：hydvs@tvcdrlbs.biz.cn

Zhù zhǐ: Shàn Lí Hè Hēilóngjiāng Shěng Hè Gǎng Shì Xìngān Qū Róng Tíng Lù 962 Hào Qǐ Zhuō Yǒuxiàn Gōngsī (Yóuzhèng Biānmǎ: 541402). Liánxì Diànhuà: 84588533. Diànzǐ Yóuxiāng: hydvs@tvcdrlbs.biz.cn

Li He Shan, Qi Zhuo Corporation, 962 Rong Ting Road, Xingan District, Hegang, Heilongjiang. Postal Code: 541402. Phone Number: 84588533. E-mail: hydvs@tvcdrlbs.biz.cn

624。姓名: 终毅仲

住址（博物院）：黑龙江省鹤岗市兴山区亭先路 976 号鹤岗博物馆（邮政编码：154800）。联系电话：61634375。电子邮箱：cxbfw@rcpzgyav.museums.cn

Zhù zhǐ: Zhōng Yì Zhòng Hēilóngjiāng Shěng Hè Gǎng Shì Xìng Shānqū Tíng Xiān Lù 976 Hào Hè Gǎng Bó Wù Guǎn (Yóuzhèng Biānmǎ: 154800). Liánxì Diànhuà: 61634375. Diànzǐ Yóuxiāng: cxbfw@rcpzgyav.museums.cn

Yi Zhong Zhong, Hegang Museum, 976 Ting Xian Road, Xingshan District, Hegang, Heilongjiang. Postal Code: 154800. Phone Number: 61634375. E-mail: cxbfw@rcpzgyav.museums.cn

625。姓名: 卓世勇

住址（公园）：黑龙江省鸡西市虎林市跃桥路 290 号食进公园（邮政编码：789893）。联系电话：22510219。电子邮箱：wfoiu@ocnwlpfb.parks.cn

Zhù zhǐ: Zhuó Shì Yǒng Hēilóngjiāng Shěng Jīxī Shì Hǔ Lín Shì Yuè Qiáo Lù 290 Hào Sì Jìn Gōng Yuán (Yóuzhèng Biānmǎ: 789893). Liánxì Diànhuà: 22510219. Diànzǐ Yóuxiāng: wfoiu@ocnwlpfb.parks.cn

Shi Yong Zhuo, Si Jin Park, 290 Yue Qiao Road, Hulin City, Jixi, Heilongjiang. Postal Code: 789893. Phone Number: 22510219. E-mail: wfoiu@ocnwlpfb.parks.cn

626。姓名: 仲孙陆中

住址（医院）：黑龙江省佳木斯市桦川县兵大路 625 号游盛医院（邮政编码：268120）。联系电话：87346339。电子邮箱：tvpbh@vzrmhdnb.health.cn

Zhù zhǐ: Zhòngsūn Liù Zhòng Hēilóngjiāng Shěng Jiāmùsī Shì Huà Chuān Xiàn Bīng Dà Lù 625 Hào Yóu Chéng Yī Yuàn (Yóuzhèng Biānmǎ: 268120). Liánxì Diànhuà: 87346339. Diànzǐ Yóuxiāng: tvpbh@vzrmhdnb.health.cn

Liu Zhong Zhongsun, You Cheng Hospital, 625 Bing Da Road, Huachuan County, Jiamusi, Heilongjiang. Postal Code: 268120. Phone Number: 87346339. E-mail: tvpbh@vzrmhdnb.health.cn

627。姓名: 荣水不

住址（机场）：黑龙江省双鸭山市岭东区坡超路 303 号双鸭山兆国国际机场（邮政编码：703945）。联系电话：83234179。电子邮箱：shkcq@qjscnzeg.airports.cn

Zhù zhǐ: Róng Shuǐ Bù Hēilóngjiāng Shěng Shuāngyāshān Shì Lǐng Dōngqū Pō Chāo Lù 303 Hào uāngyāsān Zhào Guó Guó Jì Jī Chǎng （Yóuzhèng Biānmǎ：703945）. Liánxì Diànhuà：83234179. Diànzǐ Yóuxiāng：shkcq@qjscnzeg.airports.cn

Shui Bu Rong, Shuangyashan Zhao Guo International Airport, 303 Po Chao Road, Lingdong District, Shuangyashan, Heilongjiang. Postal Code: 703945. Phone Number：83234179. E-mail：shkcq@qjscnzeg.airports.cn

628。姓名: 仇督可科

住址（机场）：黑龙江省黑河市孙吴县晗鹤路 396 号黑河黎轼国际机场（邮政编码：278109）。联系电话：32895400。电子邮箱：vwgnf@tfunkhgr.airports.cn

Zhù zhǐ: Zhǎngdū Kě Kē Hēilóngjiāng Shěng Hēihé Shì Sūn Wúxiàn Hán Hè Lù 396 Hào Hēié Lí Shì Guó Jì Jī Chǎng （Yóuzhèng Biānmǎ：278109）. Liánxì Diànhuà：32895400. Diànzǐ Yóuxiāng：vwgnf@tfunkhgr.airports.cn

Ke Ke Zhangdu, Heihe Li Shi International Airport, 396 Han He Road, Sun Wu County, Heihe, Heilongjiang. Postal Code: 278109. Phone Number：32895400. E-mail：vwgnf@tfunkhgr.airports.cn

629。姓名: 傅澜熔

住址（火车站）：黑龙江省黑河市逊克县白人路 638 号黑河站（邮政编码：352940）。联系电话：64617718。电子邮箱：pcrib@pqtkswan.chr.cn

Zhù zhǐ: Fù Lán Róng Hēilóngjiāng Shěng Hēihé Shì Xùn Kè Xiàn Bái Rén Lù 638 Hào Hēié Zhàn （Yóuzhèng Biānmǎ：352940）. Liánxì Diànhuà：64617718. Diànzǐ Yóuxiāng：pcrib@pqtkswan.chr.cn

Lan Rong Fu, Heihe Railway Station, 638 Bai Ren Road, Sunk County, Heihe, Heilongjiang. Postal Code: 352940. Phone Number：64617718. E-mail：pcrib@pqtkswan.chr.cn

630。姓名: 束泽独

住址（湖泊）：黑龙江省双鸭山市宝清县化大路 989 号先征湖（邮政编码：839299）。联系电话：83609178。电子邮箱：inzkp@koyzxqcs.lakes.cn

Zhù zhǐ: Shù Zé Dú Hēilóngjiāng Shěng Shuāngyāshān Shì Bǎo Qīng Xiàn Huā Dài Lù 989 Hào Xiān Zhēng Hú (Yóuzhèng Biānmǎ: 839299). Liánxì Diànhuà: 83609178. Diànzǐ Yóuxiāng: inzkp@koyzxqcs.lakes.cn

Ze Du Shu, Xian Zheng Lake, 989 Hua Dai Road, Baoqing County, Shuangyashan, Heilongjiang. Postal Code: 839299. Phone Number: 83609178. E-mail: inzkp@koyzxqcs.lakes.cn

631。姓名: 史熔仲

住址（医院）： 黑龙江省双鸭山市饶河县焯鹤路 777 号化辉医院（邮政编码：181260）。联系电话：65936612。电子邮箱：xquez@vprmdezb.health.cn

Zhù zhǐ: Shǐ Róng Zhòng Hēilóngjiāng Shěng Shuāngyāshān Shì Ráo Hé Xiàn Zhuō Hè Lù 777 Hào Huà Huī Yī Yuàn（Yóuzhèng Biānmǎ：181260). Liánxì Diànhuà：65936612. Diànzǐ Yóuxiāng：xquez@vprmdezb.health.cn

Rong Zhong Shi, Hua Hui Hospital, 777 Zhuo He Road, Raohe County, Shuangyashan, Heilongjiang. Postal Code: 181260. Phone Number：65936612. E-mail：xquez@vprmdezb.health.cn

632。姓名: 尹葆全

住址（公园）： 黑龙江省鹤岗市兴安区磊盛路 508 号歧陶公园（邮政编码：873208）。联系电话：50495163。电子邮箱：vkiyx@wrbkqaty.parks.cn

Zhù zhǐ: Yǐn Bǎo Quán Hēilóngjiāng Shěng Hè Gǎng Shì Xìngān Qū Lěi Chéng Lù 508 Hào Qí Táo Gōng Yuán（Yóuzhèng Biānmǎ：873208). Liánxì Diànhuà：50495163. Diànzǐ Yóuxiāng：vkiyx@wrbkqaty.parks.cn

Bao Quan Yin, Qi Tao Park, 508 Lei Cheng Road, Xingan District, Hegang, Heilongjiang. Postal Code: 873208. Phone Number：50495163. E-mail：vkiyx@wrbkqaty.parks.cn

633。姓名: 时洵臻

住址（公司）： 黑龙江省齐齐哈尔市富裕县涛盛路 994 号智跃有限公司（邮政编码：757581）。联系电话：86119358。电子邮箱：falwm@nmyjofxc.biz.cn

Zhù zhǐ: Shí Xún Zhēn Hēilóngjiāng Shěng Qíqíhāěr Shì Fùyù Xiàn Tāo Shèng Lù 994 Hào Zhì Yuè Yǒuxiàn Gōngsī（Yóuzhèng Biānmǎ：757581). Liánxì Diànhuà：86119358. Diànzǐ Yóuxiāng：falwm@nmyjofxc.biz.cn

Xun Zhen Shi, Zhi Yue Corporation, 994 Tao Sheng Road, Fuyu County, Qiqihar, Heilongjiang. Postal Code: 757581. Phone Number：86119358. E-mail：falwm@nmyjofxc.biz.cn

634。姓名: 阮熔晖

住址（火车站）：黑龙江省牡丹江市穆棱市王克路 892 号牡丹江站（邮政编码：544856）。联系电话：33096770。电子邮箱：evnoc@hcpxuzmf.chr.cn

Zhù zhǐ: Ruǎn Róng Huī Hēilóngjiāng Shěng Mǔdānjiāng Shì Mù Léng Shì Wàng Kè Lù 892 Hào Mǔdānjiāng Zhàn（Yóuzhèng Biānmǎ：544856). Liánxì Diànhuà：33096770. Diànzǐ Yóuxiāng：evnoc@hcpxuzmf.chr.cn

Rong Hui Ruan, Mudanjiang Railway Station, 892 Wang Ke Road, Mulen, Mudanjiang, Heilongjiang. Postal Code: 544856. Phone Number：33096770. E-mail：evnoc@hcpxuzmf.chr.cn

635。姓名: 家彬汉

住址（博物院）：黑龙江省鹤岗市南山区钢俊路 327 号鹤岗博物馆（邮政编码：617761）。联系电话：24158455。电子邮箱：cbofz@bduxwrvj.museums.cn

Zhù zhǐ: Jiā Bīn Hàn Hēilóngjiāng Shěng Hè Gǎng Shì Nánshānqū Gāng Jùn Lù 327 Hào Hè Gǎng Bó Wù Guǎn（Yóuzhèng Biānmǎ：617761). Liánxì Diànhuà：24158455. Diànzǐ Yóuxiāng：cbofz@bduxwrvj.museums.cn

Bin Han Jia, Hegang Museum, 327 Gang Jun Road, Nanshan District, Hegang, Heilongjiang. Postal Code: 617761. Phone Number：24158455. E-mail：cbofz@bduxwrvj.museums.cn

636。姓名: 公冶源咚

住址（大学）：黑龙江省大庆市肇源县人骥大学祥星路 399 号（邮政编码：704817）。联系电话：16782291。电子邮箱：fnaoj@ipontkev.edu.cn

Zhù zhǐ: Gōngyě Yuán Dōng Hēilóngjiāng Shěng Dàqìng Shì Zhào Yuán Xiàn Rén Jì DàxuéXiáng Xīng Lù 399 Hào（Yóuzhèng Biānmǎ：704817). Liánxì Diànhuà：16782291. Diànzǐ Yóuxiāng：fnaoj@ipontkev.edu.cn

Yuan Dong Gongye, Ren Ji University, 399 Xiang Xing Road, Zhaoyuan County, Daqing, Heilongjiang. Postal Code: 704817. Phone Number：16782291. E-mail：fnaoj@ipontkev.edu.cn

637。姓名: 童鹤大

住址（医院）：黑龙江省齐齐哈尔市富拉尔基区祥际路 404 号冕际医院（邮政编码：360358）。联系电话：40910047。电子邮箱：rscqi@ptalugno.health.cn

Zhù zhǐ: Tóng Hè Dài Hēilóngjiāng Shěng Qíqíhāěr Shì Fù Lā Ěr Jī Qū Xiáng Jì Lù 404 Hào Miǎn Jì Yī Yuàn（Yóuzhèng Biānmǎ：360358). Liánxì Diànhuà：40910047. Diànzǐ Yóuxiāng：rscqi@ptalugno.health.cn

He Dai Tong, Mian Ji Hospital, 404 Xiang Ji Road, Fularki District, Qiqihar, Heilongjiang. Postal Code: 360358. Phone Number：40910047. E-mail：rscqi@ptalugno.health.cn

638。姓名: 羿源顺

住址（医院）：黑龙江省佳木斯市桦南县游强路 386 号游自医院（邮政编码：562555）。联系电话：40215581。电子邮箱：jhobe@kmgjubzd.health.cn

Zhù zhǐ: Yì Yuán Shùn Hēilóngjiāng Shěng Jiāmùsī Shì Huà Nán Xiàn Yóu Qiáng Lù 386 Hào Yóu Zì Yī Yuàn（Yóuzhèng Biānmǎ：562555). Liánxì Diànhuà：40215581. Diànzǐ Yóuxiāng：jhobe@kmgjubzd.health.cn

Yuan Shun Yi, You Zi Hospital, 386 You Qiang Road, Huanan County, Jiamusi, Heilongjiang. Postal Code: 562555. Phone Number：40215581. E-mail：jhobe@kmgjubzd.health.cn

639。姓名: 濮发洵

住址（火车站）：黑龙江省齐齐哈尔市克山县洵禹路 885 号齐齐哈尔站（邮政编码：623368）。联系电话：40051683。电子邮箱：kopcl@fqihduzt.chr.cn

Zhù zhǐ: Pú Fā Xún Hēilóngjiāng Shěng Qíqíhāěr Shì Kè Shān Xiàn Xún Yǔ Lù 885 Hào Qíqíāěr Zhàn（Yóuzhèng Biānmǎ：623368). Liánxì Diànhuà：40051683. Diànzǐ Yóuxiāng：kopcl@fqihduzt.chr.cn

Fa Xun Pu, Qiqihar Railway Station, 885 Xun Yu Road, Keshan County, Qiqihar, Heilongjiang. Postal Code: 623368. Phone Number：40051683. E-mail：kopcl@fqihduzt.chr.cn

640。姓名: 冀鹤易

住址（家庭）：黑龙江省大庆市龙凤区征员路 907 号龙顺公寓 30 层 902 室（邮政编码：977562）。联系电话：44355631。电子邮箱：lnuji@uqwpkedr.cn

Zhù zhǐ: Jì Hè Yì Hēilóngjiāng Shěng Dàqìng Shì Lóngfèng Qū Zhēng Yún Lù 907 Hào Lóng Shùn Gōng Yù 30 Céng 902 Shì (Yóuzhèng Biānmǎ：977562). Liánxì Diànhuà：44355631. Diànzǐ Yóuxiāng：lnuji@uqwpkedr.cn

He Yi Ji, Room# 902, Floor# 30, Long Shun Apartment, 907 Zheng Yun Road, Longfeng District, Daqing, Heilongjiang. Postal Code: 977562. Phone Number：44355631. E-mail：lnuji@uqwpkedr.cn

641。姓名: 薄学葛

住址（家庭）：黑龙江省大兴安岭地区松岭区红甫路 561 号岐先公寓 49 层 336 室（邮政编码：563116）。联系电话：91966865。电子邮箱：mejlt@srntcpye.cn

Zhù zhǐ: Bó Xué Gé Hēilóngjiāng Shěng Dàxīngānlǐng Dìqū Sōng Lǐng Qū Hóng Fǔ Lù 561 Hào Qí Xiān Gōng Yù 49 Céng 336 Shì (Yóuzhèng Biānmǎ：563116). Liánxì Diànhuà：91966865. Diànzǐ Yóuxiāng：mejlt@srntcpye.cn

Xue Ge Bo, Room# 336, Floor# 49, Qi Xian Apartment, 561 Hong Fu Road, Songling District, Da Hinggan Ling, Heilongjiang. Postal Code: 563116. Phone Number：91966865. E-mail：mejlt@srntcpye.cn

642。姓名: 晏伦晗

住址（公司）：黑龙江省七台河市勃利县洵来路 957 号克世有限公司（邮政编码：410825）。联系电话：97233973。电子邮箱：ouaei@zmdxhrut.biz.cn

Zhù zhǐ: Yàn Lún Hán Hēilóngjiāng Shěng Qī Tái Hé Shì Bó Lì Xiàn Xún Lái Lù 957 Hào Kè Shì Yǒuxiàn Gōngsī (Yóuzhèng Biānmǎ：410825). Liánxì Diànhuà：97233973. Diànzǐ Yóuxiāng：ouaei@zmdxhrut.biz.cn

Lun Han Yan, Ke Shi Corporation, 957 Xun Lai Road, Burleigh County, Qitaihe, Heilongjiang. Postal Code: 410825. Phone Number：97233973. E-mail：ouaei@zmdxhrut.biz.cn

643。姓名: 楚跃世

住址（寺庙）：黑龙江省大庆市萨尔图区辙独路 897 号歧九寺（邮政编码：192758）。联系电话：15633868。电子邮箱：mwszd@pyirouhz.god.cn

Zhù zhǐ: Chǔ Yuè Shì Hēilóngjiāng Shěng Dàqìng Shì Sà Ěr Tú Qū Zhé Dú Lù 897 Hào Qí Jiǔ Sì (Yóuzhèng Biānmǎ：192758). Liánxì Diànhuà：15633868. Diànzǐ Yóuxiāng：mwszd@pyirouhz.god.cn

Yue Shi Chu, Qi Jiu Temple, 897 Zhe Du Road, Saltu District, Daqing, Heilongjiang. Postal Code: 192758. Phone Number：15633868. E-mail：mwszd@pyirouhz.god.cn

644。姓名: 柳进炯

住址（机场）：黑龙江省七台河市茄子河区独民路 877 号七台河泽屹国际机场（邮政编码：702791）。联系电话：61226217。电子邮箱：hpsyg@igslurco.airports.cn

Zhù zhǐ: Liǔ Jìn Jiǒng Hēilóngjiāng Shěng Qī Tái Hé Shì Qiézi Hé Qū Dú Mín Lù 877 Hào Qī Tái Hé Zé Yì Guó Jì Jī Chǎng (Yóuzhèng Biānmǎ：702791). Liánxì Diànhuà：61226217. Diànzǐ Yóuxiāng：hpsyg@igslurco.airports.cn

Jin Jiong Liu, Qitaihe Ze Yi International Airport, 877 Du Min Road, Eggplant River District, Qitaihe, Heilongjiang. Postal Code: 702791. Phone Number：61226217. E-mail：hpsyg@igslurco.airports.cn

645。姓名: 郁民食

住址（博物院）：黑龙江省齐齐哈尔市富拉尔基区冕甫路 200 号齐齐哈尔博物馆（邮政编码：726273）。联系电话：64961929。电子邮箱：bnscm@yqxdomhv.museums.cn

Zhù zhǐ: Yù Mín Sì Hēilóngjiāng Shěng Qíqíhāěr Shì Fù Lā Ěr Jī Qū Miǎn Fǔ Lù 200 Hào Qíqíāěr Bó Wù Guǎn (Yóuzhèng Biānmǎ：726273). Liánxì Diànhuà：64961929. Diànzǐ Yóuxiāng：bnscm@yqxdomhv.museums.cn

Min Si Yu, Qiqihar Museum, 200 Mian Fu Road, Fularki District, Qiqihar, Heilongjiang. Postal Code: 726273. Phone Number：64961929. E-mail：bnscm@yqxdomhv.museums.cn

646。姓名: 饶九顺

住址（博物院）：黑龙江省双鸭山市岭东区毅迅路 372 号双鸭山博物馆（邮政编码：255111）。联系电话：51992412。电子邮箱：cueta@hopxyevj.museums.cn

Zhù zhǐ: Ráo Jiǔ Shùn Hēilóngjiāng Shěng Shuāngyāshān Shì Lǐng Dōngqū Yì Xùn Lù 372 Hào uāngyāsān Bó Wù Guǎn (Yóuzhèng Biānmǎ：255111). Liánxì Diànhuà：51992412. Diànzǐ Yóuxiāng：cueta@hopxyevj.museums.cn

Jiu Shun Rao, Shuangyashan Museum, 372 Yi Xun Road, Lingdong District, Shuangyashan, Heilongjiang. Postal Code: 255111. Phone Number：51992412. E-mail：cueta@hopxyevj.museums.cn

647。姓名: 终坚进

住址（医院）：黑龙江省佳木斯市同江市友豪路 644 号可红医院（邮政编码：924824）。联系电话：97709783。电子邮箱：wujli@icpokrva.health.cn

Zhù zhǐ: Zhōng Jiān Jìn Hēilóngjiāng Shěng Jiāmùsī Shì Tóng Jiāng Shì Yǒu Háo Lù 644 Hào Kě Hóng Yī Yuàn (Yóuzhèng Biānmǎ：924824). Liánxì Diànhuà：97709783. Diànzǐ Yóuxiāng：wujli@icpokrva.health.cn

Jian Jin Zhong, Ke Hong Hospital, 644 You Hao Road, Tongjiang City, Jiamusi, Heilongjiang. Postal Code: 924824. Phone Number：97709783. E-mail：wujli@icpokrva.health.cn

648。姓名: 哈钦王

住址（博物院）：黑龙江省牡丹江市穆棱市发九路 253 号牡丹江博物馆（邮政编码：871709）。联系电话：76352204。电子邮箱：hgfro@jdoyklge.museums.cn

Zhù zhǐ: Hǎ Qīn Wàng Hēilóngjiāng Shěng Mǔdānjiāng Shì Mù Léng Shì Fā Jiǔ Lù 253 Hào Mǔdānjiāng Bó Wù Guǎn（Yóuzhèng Biānmǎ：871709). Liánxì Diànhuà：76352204. Diànzǐ Yóuxiāng：hgfro@jdoyklge.museums.cn

Qin Wang Ha, Mudanjiang Museum, 253 Fa Jiu Road, Mulen, Mudanjiang, Heilongjiang. Postal Code: 871709. Phone Number：76352204. E-mail：hgfro@jdoyklge.museums.cn

649。姓名: 鱼宽锤

住址（机场）：黑龙江省伊春市嘉荫县珂辙路 972 号伊春铁亚国际机场（邮政编码：609528）。联系电话：23256759。电子邮箱：tlzsq@afmjtuzn.airports.cn

Zhù zhǐ: Yú Kuān Chuí Hēilóngjiāng Shěng Yī Chūn Shì Jiā Yīn Xiàn Kē Zhé Lù 972 Hào Yī Cūn Fū Yà Guó Jì Jī Chǎng（Yóuzhèng Biānmǎ：609528). Liánxì Diànhuà：23256759. Diànzǐ Yóuxiāng：tlzsq@afmjtuzn.airports.cn

Kuan Chui Yu, Yichun Fu Ya International Airport, 972 Ke Zhe Road, Jiayin County, Yichun, Heilongjiang. Postal Code: 609528. Phone Number：23256759. E-mail： tlzsq@afmjtuzn.airports.cn

650。姓名: 邬来寰

住址（机场）：黑龙江省七台河市新兴区昌冕路 926 号七台河帆焯国际机场（邮政编码：679093）。联系电话：59197915。电子邮箱：udfje@yeagtmjw.airports.cn

Zhù zhǐ: Wū Lái Huán Hēilóngjiāng Shěng Qī Tái Hé Shì Xīnxīng Qū Chāng Miǎn Lù 926 Hào Qī Tái Hé Fān Chāo Guó Jì Jī Chǎng（Yóuzhèng Biānmǎ：679093). Liánxì Diànhuà：59197915. Diànzǐ Yóuxiāng：udfje@yeagtmjw.airports.cn

Lai Huan Wu, Qitaihe Fan Chao International Airport, 926 Chang Mian Road, Xinxing District, Qitaihe, Heilongjiang. Postal Code: 679093. Phone Number：59197915. E-mail： udfje@yeagtmjw.airports.cn

651。姓名: 微圣柱

住址（机场）：黑龙江省齐齐哈尔市克东县独乐路 528 号齐齐哈尔敬继国际机场（邮政编码：224600）。联系电话：97318499。电子邮箱：vnyfd@ksvdaety.airports.cn

Zhù zhǐ: Wēi Shèng Zhù Hēilóngjiāng Shěng Qíqíhāěr Shì Kè Dōng Xiàn Dú Lè Lù 528 Hào Qíqíāěr Jìng Jì Guó Jì Jī Chǎng (Yóuzhèng Biānmǎ: 224600). Liánxì Diànhuà: 97318499. Diànzǐ Yóuxiāng: vnyfd@ksvdaety.airports.cn

Sheng Zhu Wei, Qiqihar Jing Ji International Airport, 528 Du Le Road, Kedong County, Qiqihar, Heilongjiang. Postal Code: 224600. Phone Number: 97318499. E-mail: vnyfd@ksvdaety.airports.cn

652。姓名: 汝辉尚

住址（公司）：黑龙江省绥化市绥棱县王豹路 882 号胜骥有限公司（邮政编码：503888）。联系电话：68633712。电子邮箱：chlqf@lnribjvk.biz.cn

Zhù zhǐ: Rǔ Huī Shàng Hēilóngjiāng Shěng Suíhuà Shì Suí Léng Xiàn Wàng Bào Lù 882 Hào Shēng Jì Yǒuxiàn Gōngsī (Yóuzhèng Biānmǎ: 503888). Liánxì Diànhuà: 68633712. Diànzǐ Yóuxiāng: chlqf@lnribjvk.biz.cn

Hui Shang Ru, Sheng Ji Corporation, 882 Wang Bao Road, Suiling County, Suihua, Heilongjiang. Postal Code: 503888. Phone Number: 68633712. E-mail: chlqf@lnribjvk.biz.cn

653。姓名: 诸葛锤刚

住址（机场）：黑龙江省伊春市伊美区渊兆路 758 号伊春腾炯国际机场（邮政编码：849490）。联系电话：79025194。电子邮箱：olrae@wsmadlze.airports.cn

Zhù zhǐ: Zhūgě Chuí Gāng Hēilóngjiāng Shěng Yī Chūn Shì Yīměi Qū Yuān Zhào Lù 758 Hào Yī Cūn Téng Jiǒng Guó Jì Jī Chǎng (Yóuzhèng Biānmǎ: 849490). Liánxì Diànhuà: 79025194. Diànzǐ Yóuxiāng: olrae@wsmadlze.airports.cn

Chui Gang Zhuge, Yichun Teng Jiong International Airport, 758 Yuan Zhao Road, Immi District, Yichun, Heilongjiang. Postal Code: 849490. Phone Number: 79025194. E-mail: olrae@wsmadlze.airports.cn

654。姓名: 扈己九

住址（公司）：黑龙江省伊春市友好区兵民路 223 号陆帆有限公司（邮政编码：563276）。联系电话：93769158。电子邮箱：qmxez@klswqjdc.biz.cn

Zhù zhǐ: Hù Jǐ Jiǔ Hēilóngjiāng Shěng Yī Chūn Shì Yǒuhǎo Qū Bīng Mín Lù 223 Hào Liù Fān Yǒuxiàn Gōngsī (Yóuzhèng Biānmǎ：563276). Liánxì Diànhuà：93769158. Diànzǐ Yóuxiāng：qmxez@klswqjdc.biz.cn

Ji Jiu Hu, Liu Fan Corporation, 223 Bing Min Road, Friendly Zone, Yichun, Heilongjiang. Postal Code: 563276. Phone Number：93769158. E-mail：qmxez@klswqjdc.biz.cn

655。姓名: 鲜于光近

住址（大学）：黑龙江省双鸭山市四方台区水游大学臻计路 133 号（邮政编码：929489）。联系电话：85096917。电子邮箱：rufot@rancjptb.edu.cn

Zhù zhǐ: Xiānyú Guāng Jìn Hēilóngjiāng Shěng Shuāngyāshān Shì Sìfāng Tái Qū Shuǐ Yóu DàxuéZhēn Jì Lù 133 Hào (Yóuzhèng Biānmǎ：929489). Liánxì Diànhuà：85096917. Diànzǐ Yóuxiāng：rufot@rancjptb.edu.cn

Guang Jin Xianyu, Shui You University, 133 Zhen Ji Road, Sifangtai District, Shuangyashan, Heilongjiang. Postal Code: 929489. Phone Number：85096917. E-mail：rufot@rancjptb.edu.cn

656。姓名: 符庆葆

住址（广场）：黑龙江省哈尔滨市巴彦县豪豪路 630 号人铁广场（邮政编码：332754）。联系电话：13349114。电子邮箱：vjdic@ojtcimnb.squares.cn

Zhù zhǐ: Fú Qìng Bǎo Hēilóngjiāng Shěng Hāěrbīn Shì Bā Yàn Xiàn Háo Háo Lù 630 Hào Rén Fū Guǎng Chǎng (Yóuzhèng Biānmǎ：332754). Liánxì Diànhuà：13349114. Diànzǐ Yóuxiāng：vjdic@ojtcimnb.squares.cn

Qing Bao Fu, Ren Fu Square, 630 Hao Hao Road, Bayan County, Harbin, Heilongjiang. Postal Code: 332754. Phone Number：13349114. E-mail：vjdic@ojtcimnb.squares.cn

657。姓名: 夏其盛

住址（火车站）：黑龙江省双鸭山市集贤县化食路 391 号双鸭山站（邮政编码：639781）。联系电话：91843954。电子邮箱：whzpd@zbjtaesq.chr.cn

Zhù zhǐ: Xià Qí Shèng Hēilóngjiāng Shěng Shuāngyāshān Shì Jí Xián Xiàn Huā Shí Lù 391 Hào uāngyāsān Zhàn（Yóuzhèng Biānmǎ：639781). Liánxì Diànhuà：91843954. Diànzǐ Yóuxiāng：whzpd@zbjtaesq.chr.cn

Qi Sheng Xia, Shuangyashan Railway Station, 391 Hua Shi Road, Jixian County, Shuangyashan, Heilongjiang. Postal Code: 639781. Phone Number：91843954. E-mail：whzpd@zbjtaesq.chr.cn

658。姓名：仲孙骥大

住址（酒店）：黑龙江省伊春市金林区员惟路 492 号领楚酒店（邮政编码：269434）。联系电话：78599755。电子邮箱：xtbyq@afmbcdun.biz.cn

Zhù zhǐ: Zhòngsūn Jì Dà Hēilóngjiāng Shěng Yī Chūn Shì Jīn Lín Qū Yún Wéi Lù 492 Hào Lǐng Chǔ Jiǔ Diàn（Yóuzhèng Biānmǎ：269434). Liánxì Diànhuà：78599755. Diànzǐ Yóuxiāng：xtbyq@afmbcdun.biz.cn

Ji Da Zhongsun, Ling Chu Hotel, 492 Yun Wei Road, Jinlin District, Yichun, Heilongjiang. Postal Code: 269434. Phone Number：78599755. E-mail：xtbyq@afmbcdun.biz.cn

659。姓名：温泽奎

住址（寺庙）：黑龙江省鸡西市虎林市来德路 998 号洵炯寺（邮政编码：263769）。联系电话：30398464。电子邮箱：hyrcg@zdhqyojw.god.cn

Zhù zhǐ: Wēn Zé Kuí Hēilóngjiāng Shěng Jīxī Shì Hǔ Lín Shì Lái Dé Lù 998 Hào Xún Jiǒng Sì（Yóuzhèng Biānmǎ：263769). Liánxì Diànhuà：30398464. Diànzǐ Yóuxiāng：hyrcg@zdhqyojw.god.cn

Ze Kui Wen, Xun Jiong Temple, 998 Lai De Road, Hulin City, Jixi, Heilongjiang. Postal Code: 263769. Phone Number：30398464. E-mail：hyrcg@zdhqyojw.god.cn

660。姓名：申屠际红

住址（公园）：黑龙江省牡丹江市阳明区福源路 616 号臻晖公园（邮政编码：670513）。联系电话：24459749。电子邮箱：xrwgp@xacjhrbu.parks.cn

Zhù zhǐ: Shēntú Jì Hóng Hēilóngjiāng Shěng Mǔdānjiāng Shì Yáng Míng Qū Fú Yuán Lù 616 Hào Zhēn Huī Gōng Yuán (Yóuzhèng Biānmǎ: 670513). Liánxì Diànhuà: 24459749. Diànzǐ Yóuxiāng: xrwgp@xacjhrbu.parks.cn

Ji Hong Shentu, Zhen Hui Park, 616 Fu Yuan Road, Yangming District, Mudanjiang, Heilongjiang. Postal Code: 670513. Phone Number: 24459749. E-mail: xrwgp@xacjhrbu.parks.cn

CHAPTER 3: NAMES & LOCATIONS (61-90)

661。姓名: 闻居学

住址（公园）：黑龙江省鹤岗市工农区骥胜路 221 号铁队公园（邮政编码：633177）。联系电话：56650767。电子邮箱：klfbo@wxqgkncv.parks.cn

Zhù zhǐ: Wén Jū Xué Hēilóngjiāng Shěng Hè Gǎng Shì Gōngnóng Qū Jì Shēng Lù 221 Hào Fū Duì Gōng Yuán (Yóuzhèng Biānmǎ：633177). Liánxì Diànhuà：56650767. Diànzǐ Yóuxiāng：klfbo@wxqgkncv.parks.cn

Ju Xue Wen, Fu Dui Park, 221 Ji Sheng Road, Industrial And Agricultural Area, Hegang, Heilongjiang. Postal Code: 633177. Phone Number：56650767. E-mail：klfbo@wxqgkncv.parks.cn

662。姓名: 訾轼惟

住址（酒店）：黑龙江省牡丹江市林口县茂愈路 321 号焯风酒店（邮政编码：559824）。联系电话：65079031。电子邮箱：avtbk@rdpycakn.biz.cn

Zhù zhǐ: Zǐ Shì Wéi Hēilóngjiāng Shěng Mǔdānjiāng Shì Línkǒu Xiàn Mào Yù Lù 321 Hào Zhuō Fēng Jiǔ Diàn (Yóuzhèng Biānmǎ：559824). Liánxì Diànhuà：65079031. Diànzǐ Yóuxiāng：avtbk@rdpycakn.biz.cn

Shi Wei Zi, Zhuo Feng Hotel, 321 Mao Yu Road, Linkou County, Mudanjiang, Heilongjiang. Postal Code: 559824. Phone Number：65079031. E-mail：avtbk@rdpycakn.biz.cn

663。姓名: 哈全迅

住址（大学）：黑龙江省伊春市南岔县可翰大学亭庆路 703 号（邮政编码：181115）。联系电话：39754629。电子邮箱：apogb@jmxygvlz.edu.cn

Zhù zhǐ: Hǎ Quán Xùn Hēilóngjiāng Shěng Yī Chūn Shì Nán Chà Xiàn Kě Hàn Dàxué Tíng Qìng Lù 703 Hào (Yóuzhèng Biānmǎ：181115). Liánxì Diànhuà：39754629. Diànzǐ Yóuxiāng：apogb@jmxygvlz.edu.cn

Quan Xun Ha, Ke Han University, 703 Ting Qing Road, Nancha County, Yichun, Heilongjiang. Postal Code: 181115. Phone Number：39754629. E-mail：apogb@jmxygvlz.edu.cn

664。姓名: 梁丘中钦

住址（公共汽车站）：黑龙江省鸡西市滴道区谢臻路 210 号发智站（邮政编码：515705）。联系电话：80973972。电子邮箱：boyfn@aidwkzfu.transport.cn

Zhù zhǐ: Liángqiū Zhōng Qīn Hēilóngjiāng Shěng Jīxī Shì Dī Dào Qū Xiè Zhēn Lù 210 Hào Fā Zhì Zhàn （Yóuzhèng Biānmǎ：515705). Liánxì Diànhuà：80973972. Diànzǐ Yóuxiāng: boyfn@aidwkzfu.transport.cn

Zhong Qin Liangqiu, Fa Zhi Bus Station, 210 Xie Zhen Road, Didao District, Jixi, Heilongjiang. Postal Code: 515705. Phone Number：80973972. E-mail：boyfn@aidwkzfu.transport.cn

665。姓名: 郑桥圣

住址（公司）：黑龙江省佳木斯市富锦市陆大路 872 号尚光有限公司（邮政编码：851131）。联系电话：32837888。电子邮箱：dxjhs@ubinqamg.biz.cn

Zhù zhǐ: Zhèng Qiáo Shèng Hēilóngjiāng Shěng Jiāmùsī Shì Fù Jǐn Shì Liù Dà Lù 872 Hào Shàng Guāng Yǒuxiàn Gōngsī （Yóuzhèng Biānmǎ：851131). Liánxì Diànhuà：32837888. Diànzǐ Yóuxiāng：dxjhs@ubinqamg.biz.cn

Qiao Sheng Zheng, Shang Guang Corporation, 872 Liu Da Road, Fujin, Jiamusi, Heilongjiang. Postal Code: 851131. Phone Number：32837888. E-mail：dxjhs@ubinqamg.biz.cn

666。姓名: 竺坚智

住址（公司）：黑龙江省大庆市让胡路区澜近路 374 号近居有限公司（邮政编码：951559）。联系电话：19144939。电子邮箱：cjgki@suhcxotz.biz.cn

Zhù zhǐ: Zhú Jiān Zhì Hēilóngjiāng Shěng Dàqìng Shì Ràng Hú Lù Qū Lán Jìn Lù 374 Hào Jìn Jū Yǒuxiàn Gōngsī （Yóuzhèng Biānmǎ：951559). Liánxì Diànhuà：19144939. Diànzǐ Yóuxiāng：cjgki@suhcxotz.biz.cn

Jian Zhi Zhu, Jin Ju Corporation, 374 Lan Jin Road, Ranghu Road District, Daqing, Heilongjiang. Postal Code: 951559. Phone Number：19144939. E-mail：cjgki@suhcxotz.biz.cn

667。姓名: 王甫尚

住址（寺庙）：黑龙江省哈尔滨市延寿县易屹路 971 号俊人寺（邮政编码：688189）。联系电话：48035683。电子邮箱：lcqkx@yxpkhuwt.god.cn

Zhù zhǐ: Wáng Fǔ Shàng Hēilóngjiāng Shěng Hāěrbīn Shì Yánshòu Xiàn Yì Yì Lù 971 Hào Jùn Rén Sì（Yóuzhèng Biānmǎ：688189). Liánxì Diànhuà：48035683. Diànzǐ Yóuxiāng：lcqkx@yxpkhuwt.god.cn

Fu Shang Wang, Jun Ren Temple, 971 Yi Yi Road, Yanshou County, Harbin, Heilongjiang. Postal Code: 688189. Phone Number：48035683. E-mail：lcqkx@yxpkhuwt.god.cn

668。姓名: 呼延舟钊

住址（医院）：黑龙江省绥化市明水县仲星路 495 号楚淹医院（邮政编码：458122）。联系电话：15387437。电子邮箱：oexgm@tgruvcoz.health.cn

Zhù zhǐ: Hūyán Zhōu Zhāo Hēilóngjiāng Shěng Suíhuà Shì Míng Shuǐ Xiàn Zhòng Xīng Lù 495 Hào Chǔ Yān Yī Yuàn（Yóuzhèng Biānmǎ：458122). Liánxì Diànhuà：15387437. Diànzǐ Yóuxiāng：oexgm@tgruvcoz.health.cn

Zhou Zhao Huyan, Chu Yan Hospital, 495 Zhong Xing Road, Mingshui County, Suihua, Heilongjiang. Postal Code: 458122. Phone Number：15387437. E-mail：oexgm@tgruvcoz.health.cn

669。姓名: 宰进强

住址（机场）：黑龙江省大庆市大同区亚浩路 493 号大庆钢独国际机场（邮政编码：865184）。联系电话：26037306。电子邮箱：tdzxe@wfcijrmb.airports.cn

Zhù zhǐ: Zǎi Jìn Qiǎng Hēilóngjiāng Shěng Dàqìng Shì Dàtóng Qū Yà Hào Lù 493 Hào Dàqng Gāng Dú Guó Jì Jī Chǎng（Yóuzhèng Biānmǎ：865184). Liánxì Diànhuà：26037306. Diànzǐ Yóuxiāng：tdzxe@wfcijrmb.airports.cn

Jin Qiang Zai, Daqing Gang Du International Airport, 493 Ya Hao Road, Datong District, Daqing, Heilongjiang. Postal Code: 865184. Phone Number：26037306. E-mail：tdzxe@wfcijrmb.airports.cn

670。姓名: 逯大食

住址（公司）：黑龙江省大庆市林甸县敬友路 804 号福维有限公司（邮政编码：455127）。联系电话：19992004。电子邮箱：kahcv@cwbyzhmk.biz.cn

Zhù zhǐ: Lù Dà Shí Hēilóngjiāng Shěng Dàqìng Shì Lín Diānxiàn Jìng Yǒu Lù 804 Hào Fú Wéi Yǒuxiàn Gōngsī（Yóuzhèng Biānmǎ：455127). Liánxì Diànhuà：19992004. Diànzǐ Yóuxiāng：kahcv@cwbyzhmk.biz.cn

Da Shi Lu, Fu Wei Corporation, 804 Jing You Road, Lindian County, Daqing, Heilongjiang. Postal Code: 455127. Phone Number：19992004. E-mail：kahcv@cwbyzhmk.biz.cn

671。姓名: 章豹水

住址（公共汽车站）：黑龙江省大庆市让胡路区歧秀路 622 号铭克站（邮政编码：313581）。联系电话：16052737。电子邮箱：arngo@yxrdcljp.transport.cn

Zhù zhǐ: Zhāng Bào Shuǐ Hēilóngjiāng Shěng Dàqìng Shì Ràng Hú Lù Qū Qí Xiù Lù 622 Hào Míng Kè Zhàn（Yóuzhèng Biānmǎ：313581). Liánxì Diànhuà：16052737. Diànzǐ Yóuxiāng：arngo@yxrdcljp.transport.cn

Bao Shui Zhang, Ming Ke Bus Station, 622 Qi Xiu Road, Ranghu Road District, Daqing, Heilongjiang. Postal Code: 313581. Phone Number：16052737. E-mail：arngo@yxrdcljp.transport.cn

672。姓名: 富涛白

住址（机场）：黑龙江省伊春市伊美区南谢路 739 号伊春钊易国际机场（邮政编码：987555）。联系电话：61582231。电子邮箱：wzrnu@uejqysot.airports.cn

Zhù zhǐ: Fù Tāo Bái Hēilóngjiāng Shěng Yī Chūn Shì Yīměi Qū Nán Xiè Lù 739 Hào Yī Cūn Zhāo Yì Guó Jì Jī Chǎng（Yóuzhèng Biānmǎ：987555). Liánxì Diànhuà：61582231. Diànzǐ Yóuxiāng：wzrnu@uejqysot.airports.cn

Tao Bai Fu, Yichun Zhao Yi International Airport, 739 Nan Xie Road, Immi District, Yichun, Heilongjiang. Postal Code: 987555. Phone Number：61582231. E-mail：wzrnu@uejqysot.airports.cn

673。姓名: 寇全绅

住址（家庭）：黑龙江省黑河市嫩江市锡锤路 494 号发庆公寓 30 层 727 室（邮政编码：815754）。联系电话：97882627。电子邮箱：guyia@dosmcrhy.cn

Zhù zhǐ: Kòu Quán Shēn Hēilóngjiāng Shěng Hēihé Shì Nènjiāng Shì Xī Chuí Lù 494 Hào Fā Qìng Gōng Yù 30 Céng 727 Shì (Yóuzhèng Biānmǎ：815754). Liánxì Diànhuà：97882627. Diànzǐ Yóuxiāng：guyia@dosmcrhy.cn

Quan Shen Kou, Room# 727, Floor# 30, Fa Qing Apartment, 494 Xi Chui Road, Nenjiang City, Heihe, Heilongjiang. Postal Code: 815754. Phone Number：97882627. E-mail：guyia@dosmcrhy.cn

674。姓名: 有其敬

住址（广场）：黑龙江省大庆市龙凤区院强路 850 号隆白广场（邮政编码：306660）。联系电话：47943588。电子邮箱：awgmf@ezothcjg.squares.cn

Zhù zhǐ: Yǒu Qí Jìng Hēilóngjiāng Shěng Dàqìng Shì Lóngfèng Qū Yuàn Qiǎng Lù 850 Hào Lóng Bái Guǎng Chǎng (Yóuzhèng Biānmǎ：306660). Liánxì Diànhuà：47943588. Diànzǐ Yóuxiāng：awgmf@ezothcjg.squares.cn

Qi Jing You, Long Bai Square, 850 Yuan Qiang Road, Longfeng District, Daqing, Heilongjiang. Postal Code: 306660. Phone Number：47943588. E-mail：awgmf@ezothcjg.squares.cn

675。姓名: 鲁珏禹

住址（公园）：黑龙江省齐齐哈尔市龙沙区龙焯路 391 号庆易公园（邮政编码：763450）。联系电话：53551452。电子邮箱：xbslr@dxnzuhpe.parks.cn

Zhù zhǐ: Lǔ Jué Yǔ Hēilóngjiāng Shěng Qíqíhāěr Shì Lóng Shā Qū Lóng Zhuō Lù 391 Hào Qìng Yì Gōng Yuán (Yóuzhèng Biānmǎ：763450). Liánxì Diànhuà：53551452. Diànzǐ Yóuxiāng：xbslr@dxnzuhpe.parks.cn

Jue Yu Lu, Qing Yi Park, 391 Long Zhuo Road, Longsha District, Qiqihar, Heilongjiang. Postal Code: 763450. Phone Number：53551452. E-mail：xbslr@dxnzuhpe.parks.cn

676。姓名: 邱豪豪

住址（医院）：黑龙江省绥化市海伦市土源路 691 号钢桥医院（邮政编码：180910）。联系电话：56567255。电子邮箱：obklu@lcrahxei.health.cn

Zhù zhǐ: Qiū Háo Háo Hēilóngjiāng Shěng Suíhuà Shì Hǎilún Shì Tǔ Yuán Lù 691 Hào Gāng Qiáo Yī Yuàn（Yóuzhèng Biānmǎ：180910). Liánxì Diànhuà：56567255. Diànzǐ Yóuxiāng：obklu@lcrahxei.health.cn

Hao Hao Qiu, Gang Qiao Hospital, 691 Tu Yuan Road, Helen, Suihua, Heilongjiang. Postal Code: 180910. Phone Number：56567255. E-mail：obklu@lcrahxei.health.cn

677。姓名: 陈惟九

住址（广场）：黑龙江省哈尔滨市方正县汉食路 740 号九超广场（邮政编码：819581）。联系电话：11667523。电子邮箱：mirnx@kqwsejfl.squares.cn

Zhù zhǐ: Chén Wéi Jiǔ Hēilóngjiāng Shěng Hāěrbīn Shì Fāngzhèng Xiàn Hàn Yì Lù 740 Hào Jiǔ Chāo Guǎng Chǎng（Yóuzhèng Biānmǎ：819581). Liánxì Diànhuà：11667523. Diànzǐ Yóuxiāng：mirnx@kqwsejfl.squares.cn

Wei Jiu Chen, Jiu Chao Square, 740 Han Yi Road, Fangzheng County, Harbin, Heilongjiang. Postal Code: 819581. Phone Number：11667523. E-mail：mirnx@kqwsejfl.squares.cn

678。姓名: 越钦化

住址（家庭）：黑龙江省黑河市逊克县进食路 102 号刚磊公寓 36 层 957 室（邮政编码：873751）。联系电话：98677211。电子邮箱：jyqzk@gxubcapl.cn

Zhù zhǐ: Yuè Qīn Huà Hēilóngjiāng Shěng Hēihé Shì Xùn Kè Xiàn Jìn Yì Lù 102 Hào Gāng Lěi Gōng Yù 36 Céng 957 Shì (Yóuzhèng Biānmǎ：873751). Liánxì Diànhuà：98677211. Diànzǐ Yóuxiāng：jyqzk@gxubcapl.cn

Qin Hua Yue, Room# 957, Floor# 36, Gang Lei Apartment, 102 Jin Yi Road, Sunk County, Heihe, Heilongjiang. Postal Code: 873751. Phone Number：98677211. E-mail：jyqzk@gxubcapl.cn

679。姓名: 母队沛

住址（广场）：黑龙江省齐齐哈尔市克山县石智路 590 号大渊广场（邮政编码：289745）。联系电话：35899348。电子邮箱：rdmhv@vmryzgpk.squares.cn

Zhù zhǐ: Mǔ Duì Bèi Hēilóngjiāng Shěng Qíqíhāěr Shì Kè Shān Xiàn Shí Zhì Lù 590 Hào Dà Yuān Guǎng Chǎng（Yóuzhèng Biānmǎ：289745）. Liánxì Diànhuà：35899348. Diànzǐ Yóuxiāng：rdmhv@vmryzgpk.squares.cn

Dui Bei Mu, Da Yuan Square, 590 Shi Zhi Road, Keshan County, Qiqihar, Heilongjiang. Postal Code: 289745. Phone Number：35899348. E-mail：rdmhv@vmryzgpk.squares.cn

680。姓名: 嵇铭游

住址（酒店）：黑龙江省齐齐哈尔市富裕县惟尚路 977 号乐源酒店（邮政编码：840381）。联系电话：96039092。电子邮箱：simau@miogkezc.biz.cn

Zhù zhǐ: Jī Míng Yóu Hēilóngjiāng Shěng Qíqíhāěr Shì Fùyù Xiàn Wéi Shàng Lù 977 Hào Lè Yuán Jiǔ Diàn（Yóuzhèng Biānmǎ：840381）. Liánxì Diànhuà：96039092. Diànzǐ Yóuxiāng：simau@miogkezc.biz.cn

Ming You Ji, Le Yuan Hotel, 977 Wei Shang Road, Fuyu County, Qiqihar, Heilongjiang. Postal Code: 840381. Phone Number：96039092. E-mail：simau@miogkezc.biz.cn

681。姓名: 娄队可

住址（医院）：黑龙江省佳木斯市前进区化立路 134 号坤宽医院（邮政编码：411750）。联系电话：96767154。电子邮箱：nlcrx@kwuefivc.health.cn

Zhù zhǐ: Lóu Duì Kě Hēilóngjiāng Shěng Jiāmùsī Shì Qiánjìn Qū Huà Lì Lù 134 Hào Kūn Kuān Yī Yuàn（Yóuzhèng Biānmǎ：411750）. Liánxì Diànhuà：96767154. Diànzǐ Yóuxiāng：nlcrx@kwuefivc.health.cn

Dui Ke Lou, Kun Kuan Hospital, 134 Hua Li Road, Forward Area, Jiamusi, Heilongjiang. Postal Code: 411750. Phone Number：96767154. E-mail：nlcrx@kwuefivc.health.cn

682。姓名: 潘钢岐

住址（湖泊）：黑龙江省大庆市肇源县铁食路 359 号炯咚湖（邮政编码：505914）。联系电话：28774579。电子邮箱：uvtma@kguxihyv.lakes.cn

Zhù zhǐ: Pān Gāng Qí Hēilóngjiāng Shěng Dàqìng Shì Zhào Yuán Xiàn Fū Shí Lù 359 Hào Jiǒng Dōng Hú（Yóuzhèng Biānmǎ：505914). Liánxì Diànhuà：28774579. Diànzǐ Yóuxiāng：uvtma@kguxihyv.lakes.cn

Gang Qi Pan, Jiong Dong Lake, 359 Fu Shi Road, Zhaoyuan County, Daqing, Heilongjiang. Postal Code: 505914. Phone Number：28774579. E-mail：uvtma@kguxihyv.lakes.cn

683。姓名: 谢独阳

住址（寺庙）：黑龙江省齐齐哈尔市昂昂溪区己坚路 838 号岐翰寺（邮政编码：928715）。联系电话：23674604。电子邮箱：jphex@atlniuxb.god.cn

Zhù zhǐ: Xiè Dú Yáng Hēilóngjiāng Shěng Qíqíhāěr Shì Ángáng Xī Qū Jǐ Jiān Lù 838 Hào Qí Hàn Sì（Yóuzhèng Biānmǎ：928715). Liánxì Diànhuà：23674604. Diànzǐ Yóuxiāng：jphex@atlniuxb.god.cn

Du Yang Xie, Qi Han Temple, 838 Ji Jian Road, Angang Creek District, Qiqihar, Heilongjiang. Postal Code: 928715. Phone Number：23674604. E-mail：jphex@atlniuxb.god.cn

684。姓名: 时全恩

住址（公园）：黑龙江省牡丹江市阳明区刚游路 566 号淹领公园（邮政编码：670247）。联系电话：88691857。电子邮箱：wrdox@khvepibl.parks.cn

Zhù zhǐ: Shí Quán Ēn Hēilóngjiāng Shěng Mǔdānjiāng Shì Yáng Míng Qū Gāng Yóu Lù 566 Hào Yān Lǐng Gōng Yuán（Yóuzhèng Biānmǎ：670247). Liánxì Diànhuà：88691857. Diànzǐ Yóuxiāng：wrdox@khvepibl.parks.cn

Quan En Shi, Yan Ling Park, 566 Gang You Road, Yangming District, Mudanjiang, Heilongjiang. Postal Code: 670247. Phone Number：88691857. E-mail：wrdox@khvepibl.parks.cn

685。姓名: 詹庆隆

住址（广场）：黑龙江省黑河市孙吴县涛立路 598 号鹤科广场（邮政编码：519605）。联系电话：29145802。电子邮箱：ncypa@hnzxgebm.squares.cn

Zhù zhǐ: Zhān Qìng Lóng Hēilóngjiāng Shěng Hēihé Shì Sūn Wúxiàn Tāo Lì Lù 598 Hào Hè Kē Guǎng Chǎng（Yóuzhèng Biānmǎ：519605). Liánxì Diànhuà：29145802. Diànzǐ Yóuxiāng：ncypa@hnzxgebm.squares.cn

Qing Long Zhan, He Ke Square, 598 Tao Li Road, Sun Wu County, Heihe, Heilongjiang. Postal Code: 519605. Phone Number：29145802. E-mail：ncypa@hnzxgebm.squares.cn

686。姓名: 彭骥晗

住址（湖泊）：黑龙江省双鸭山市饶河县舟坤路 826 号翰食湖（邮政编码：622371）。联系电话：13553500。电子邮箱：yswok@yejqzrom.lakes.cn

Zhù zhǐ: Péng Jì Hán Hēilóngjiāng Shěng Shuāngyāshān Shì Ráo Hé Xiàn Zhōu Kūn Lù 826 Hào Hàn Sì Hú（Yóuzhèng Biānmǎ：622371). Liánxì Diànhuà：13553500. Diànzǐ Yóuxiāng：yswok@yejqzrom.lakes.cn

Ji Han Peng, Han Si Lake, 826 Zhou Kun Road, Raohe County, Shuangyashan, Heilongjiang. Postal Code: 622371. Phone Number：13553500. E-mail：yswok@yejqzrom.lakes.cn

687。姓名: 叶秀陆

住址（公园）：黑龙江省黑河市爱辉区仓翰路 840 号强坚公园（邮政编码：132052）。联系电话：88183547。电子邮箱：vajfc@qlxyasod.parks.cn

Zhù zhǐ: Yè Xiù Lù Hēilóngjiāng Shěng Hēihé Shì Ài Huī Qū Cāng Hàn Lù 840 Hào Qiǎng Jiān Gōng Yuán（Yóuzhèng Biānmǎ：132052). Liánxì Diànhuà：88183547. Diànzǐ Yóuxiāng：vajfc@qlxyasod.parks.cn

Xiu Lu Ye, Qiang Jian Park, 840 Cang Han Road, Aihui District, Heihe, Heilongjiang. Postal Code: 132052. Phone Number：88183547. E-mail：vajfc@qlxyasod.parks.cn

688。姓名: 海彬征

住址（公共汽车站）：黑龙江省牡丹江市西安区铭俊路 679 号白恩站（邮政编码：832438）。联系电话：91694967。电子邮箱：ftlhw@rbdaocek.transport.cn

Zhù zhǐ: Hǎi Bīn Zhēng Hēilóngjiāng Shěng Mǔdānjiāng Shì Xīān Qū Míng Jùn Lù 679 Hào Bái Ēn Zhàn （Yóuzhèng Biānmǎ：832438). Liánxì Diànhuà：91694967. Diànzǐ Yóuxiāng：ftlhw@rbdaocek.transport.cn

Bin Zheng Hai, Bai En Bus Station, 679 Ming Jun Road, Xian District, Mudanjiang, Heilongjiang. Postal Code: 832438. Phone Number：91694967. E-mail：ftlhw@rbdaocek.transport.cn

689。姓名: 燕独胜

住址（湖泊）：黑龙江省大兴安岭地区漠河市继彬路 742 号征先湖（邮政编码：435394）。联系电话：86994640。电子邮箱：udokt@npwvszgc.lakes.cn

Zhù zhǐ: Yān Dú Shēng Hēilóngjiāng Shěng Dàxīngānlǐng Dìqū Mòhé Shì Jì Bīn Lù 742 Hào Zhēng Xiān Hú （Yóuzhèng Biānmǎ：435394). Liánxì Diànhuà：86994640. Diànzǐ Yóuxiāng：udokt@npwvszgc.lakes.cn

Du Sheng Yan, Zheng Xian Lake, 742 Ji Bin Road, Mohe City, Da Hinggan Ling, Heilongjiang. Postal Code: 435394. Phone Number：86994640. E-mail：udokt@npwvszgc.lakes.cn

690。姓名: 明葆豹

住址（广场）：黑龙江省七台河市勃利县迅不路 619 号辉兆广场（邮政编码：726769）。联系电话：29663675。电子邮箱：nxyot@gypzlsrm.squares.cn

Zhù zhǐ: Míng Bǎo Bào Hēilóngjiāng Shěng Qī Tái Hé Shì Bó Lì Xiàn Xùn Bù Lù 619 Hào Huī Zhào Guǎng Chǎng （Yóuzhèng Biānmǎ：726769). Liánxì Diànhuà：29663675. Diànzǐ Yóuxiāng：nxyot@gypzlsrm.squares.cn

Bao Bao Ming, Hui Zhao Square, 619 Xun Bu Road, Burleigh County, Qitaihe, Heilongjiang. Postal Code: 726769. Phone Number：29663675. E-mail：nxyot@gypzlsrm.squares.cn

CHAPTER 4: NAMES & LOCATIONS (91-120)

691。姓名: 羊稼化

住址（家庭）：黑龙江省双鸭山市宝清县星珂路 552 号鹤国公寓 6 层 629 室（邮政编码：146002）。联系电话：57203687。电子邮箱：vorij@wqtrfobe.cn

Zhù zhǐ: Yáng Jià Huà Hēilóngjiāng Shěng Shuāngyāshān Shì Bǎo Qīng Xiàn Xīng Kē Lù 552 Hào Hè Guó Gōng Yù 6 Céng 629 Shì (Yóuzhèng Biānmǎ：146002). Liánxì Diànhuà：57203687. Diànzǐ Yóuxiāng：vorij@wqtrfobe.cn

Jia Hua Yang, Room# 629, Floor# 6, He Guo Apartment, 552 Xing Ke Road, Baoqing County, Shuangyashan, Heilongjiang. Postal Code: 146002. Phone Number：57203687. E-mail：vorij@wqtrfobe.cn

692。姓名: 宰父己刚

住址（酒店）：黑龙江省牡丹江市东安区稼食路 395 号游豹酒店（邮政编码：918527）。联系电话：74066185。电子邮箱：zybar@szahcymq.biz.cn

Zhù zhǐ: Zǎifǔ Jǐ Gāng Hēilóngjiāng Shěng Mǔdānjiāng Shì Dōngān Qū Jià Yì Lù 395 Hào Yóu Bào Jiǔ Diàn (Yóuzhèng Biānmǎ：918527). Liánxì Diànhuà：74066185. Diànzǐ Yóuxiāng：zybar@szahcymq.biz.cn

Ji Gang Zaifu, You Bao Hotel, 395 Jia Yi Road, Dongan District, Mudanjiang, Heilongjiang. Postal Code: 918527. Phone Number：74066185. E-mail：zybar@szahcymq.biz.cn

693。姓名: 秦隆食

住址（公共汽车站）：黑龙江省伊春市伊美区星乙路 681 号智葆站（邮政编码：468163）。联系电话：19743153。电子邮箱：hpwre@wtqdgxum.transport.cn

Zhù zhǐ: Qín Lóng Shí Hēilóngjiāng Shěng Yī Chūn Shì Yīměi Qū Xīng Yǐ Lù 681 Hào Zhì Bǎo Zhàn (Yóuzhèng Biānmǎ：468163). Liánxì Diànhuà：19743153. Diànzǐ Yóuxiāng：hpwre@wtqdgxum.transport.cn

Long Shi Qin, Zhi Bao Bus Station, 681 Xing Yi Road, Immi District, Yichun, Heilongjiang. Postal Code: 468163. Phone Number：19743153. E-mail：hpwre@wtqdgxum.transport.cn

694。姓名: 严桥波

住址（火车站）：黑龙江省伊春市乌翠区己兆路 762 号伊春站（邮政编码：598918）。联系电话：50568642。电子邮箱：rudje@szxhmgjr.chr.cn

Zhù zhǐ: Yán Qiáo Bō Hēilóngjiāng Shěng Yī Chūn Shì Wū Cuì Qū Jǐ Zhào Lù 762 Hào Yī Cūn Zhàn (Yóuzhèng Biānmǎ：598918). Liánxì Diànhuà：50568642. Diànzǐ Yóuxiāng：rudje@szxhmgjr.chr.cn

Qiao Bo Yan, Yichun Railway Station, 762 Ji Zhao Road, Wucui District, Yichun, Heilongjiang. Postal Code: 598918. Phone Number：50568642. E-mail：rudje@szxhmgjr.chr.cn

695。姓名: 宿人磊

住址（公司）：黑龙江省绥化市兰西县迅咚路 468 号立计有限公司（邮政编码：548450）。联系电话：23329599。电子邮箱：dtmfy@kihsgdxe.biz.cn

Zhù zhǐ: Sù Rén Lěi Hēilóngjiāng Shěng Suíhuà Shì Lán Xī Xiàn Xùn Dōng Lù 468 Hào Lì Jì Yǒuxiàn Gōngsī (Yóuzhèng Biānmǎ：548450). Liánxì Diànhuà：23329599. Diànzǐ Yóuxiāng：dtmfy@kihsgdxe.biz.cn

Ren Lei Su, Li Ji Corporation, 468 Xun Dong Road, Lanxi County, Suihua, Heilongjiang. Postal Code: 548450. Phone Number：23329599. E-mail：dtmfy@kihsgdxe.biz.cn

696。姓名: 缪自食

住址（公园）：黑龙江省佳木斯市向阳区科尚路 295 号骥超公园（邮政编码：222418）。联系电话：17176981。电子邮箱：maxpf@nwflxmth.parks.cn

Zhù zhǐ: Miào Zì Yì Hēilóngjiāng Shěng Jiāmùsī Shì Xiàngyáng Qū Kē Shàng Lù 295 Hào Jì Chāo Gōng Yuán (Yóuzhèng Biānmǎ：222418). Liánxì Diànhuà：17176981. Diànzǐ Yóuxiāng：maxpf@nwflxmth.parks.cn

Zi Yi Miao, Ji Chao Park, 295 Ke Shang Road, Xiangyang District, Jiamusi, Heilongjiang. Postal Code: 222418. Phone Number：17176981. E-mail：maxpf@nwflxmth.parks.cn

697。姓名: 富乐强

住址（医院）：黑龙江省黑河市北安市自隆路 611 号奎人医院（邮政编码：994314）。联系电话：15178222。电子邮箱：uxwcm@htfscpor.health.cn

Zhù zhǐ: Fù Lè Qiáng Hēilóngjiāng Shěng Hēihé Shì Běi Ān Shì Zì Lóng Lù 611 Hào Kuí Rén Yī Yuàn（Yóuzhèng Biānmǎ：994314). Liánxì Diànhuà：15178222. Diànzǐ Yóuxiāng：uxwcm@htfscpor.health.cn

Le Qiang Fu, Kui Ren Hospital, 611 Zi Long Road, Beian, Heihe, Heilongjiang. Postal Code: 994314. Phone Number：15178222. E-mail：uxwcm@htfscpor.health.cn

698。姓名: 晋葛振

住址（湖泊）：黑龙江省鹤岗市工农区秀游路 361 号轼强湖（邮政编码：144517）。联系电话：33895467。电子邮箱：jqmin@auohcwdy.lakes.cn

Zhù zhǐ: Jìn Gé Zhèn Hēilóngjiāng Shěng Hè Gǎng Shì Gōngnóng Qū Xiù Yóu Lù 361 Hào Shì Qiǎng Hú（Yóuzhèng Biānmǎ：144517). Liánxì Diànhuà：33895467. Diànzǐ Yóuxiāng：jqmin@auohcwdy.lakes.cn

Ge Zhen Jin, Shi Qiang Lake, 361 Xiu You Road, Industrial And Agricultural Area, Hegang, Heilongjiang. Postal Code: 144517. Phone Number：33895467. E-mail：jqmin@auohcwdy.lakes.cn

699。姓名: 束乐禹

住址（家庭）：黑龙江省哈尔滨市南岗区兵龙路 374 号兵土公寓 10 层 297 室（邮政编码：729086）。联系电话：11424218。电子邮箱：ubktf@gqftuisk.cn

Zhù zhǐ: Shù Lè Yǔ Hēilóngjiāng Shěng Hāěrbīn Shì Nángǎng Qū Bīng Lóng Lù 374 Hào Bīng Tǔ Gōng Yù 10 Céng 297 Shì (Yóuzhèng Biānmǎ：729086). Liánxì Diànhuà：11424218. Diànzǐ Yóuxiāng：ubktf@gqftuisk.cn

Le Yu Shu, Room# 297, Floor# 10, Bing Tu Apartment, 374 Bing Long Road, Nangang District, Harbin, Heilongjiang. Postal Code: 729086. Phone Number：11424218. E-mail：ubktf@gqftuisk.cn

700。姓名: 阎科智

住址（医院）：黑龙江省鹤岗市工农区冠维路 887 号继焯医院（邮政编码：465530）。联系电话：44340820。电子邮箱：adhpm@wahqpujm.health.cn

Zhù zhǐ: Yán Kē Zhì Hēilóngjiāng Shěng Hè Gǎng Shì Gōngnóng Qū Guān Wéi Lù 887 Hào Jì Chāo Yī Yuàn（Yóuzhèng Biānmǎ：465530). Liánxì Diànhuà：44340820. Diànzǐ Yóuxiāng：adhpm@wahqpujm.health.cn

Ke Zhi Yan, Ji Chao Hospital, 887 Guan Wei Road, Industrial And Agricultural Area, Hegang, Heilongjiang. Postal Code: 465530. Phone Number：44340820. E-mail：adhpm@wahqpujm.health.cn

701。姓名: 施辉屹

住址（机场）：黑龙江省齐齐哈尔市甘南县晖柱路 375 号齐齐哈尔辙际国际机场（邮政编码：389048）。联系电话：60172530。电子邮箱：ubxro@iowcpzfq.airports.cn

Zhù zhǐ: Shī Huī Yì Hēilóngjiāng Shěng Qíqíhāěr Shì Gānnán Xiàn Huī Zhù Lù 375 Hào Qíqíāěr Zhé Jì Guó Jì Jī Chǎng（Yóuzhèng Biānmǎ：389048). Liánxì Diànhuà：60172530. Diànzǐ Yóuxiāng：ubxro@iowcpzfq.airports.cn

Hui Yi Shi, Qiqihar Zhe Ji International Airport, 375 Hui Zhu Road, Gannan County, Qiqihar, Heilongjiang. Postal Code: 389048. Phone Number：60172530. E-mail：ubxro@iowcpzfq.airports.cn

702。姓名: 琴风中

住址（大学）：黑龙江省绥化市兰西县中兆大学淹际路 841 号（邮政编码：897071）。联系电话：64498081。电子邮箱：zjvbp@dftguiho.edu.cn

Zhù zhǐ: Qín Fēng Zhòng Hēilóngjiāng Shěng Suíhuà Shì Lán Xī Xiàn Zhōng Zhào DàxuéYān Jì Lù 841 Hào（Yóuzhèng Biānmǎ：897071). Liánxì Diànhuà：64498081. Diànzǐ Yóuxiāng：zjvbp@dftguiho.edu.cn

Feng Zhong Qin, Zhong Zhao University, 841 Yan Ji Road, Lanxi County, Suihua, Heilongjiang. Postal Code: 897071. Phone Number：64498081. E-mail：zjvbp@dftguiho.edu.cn

703。姓名: 司空南鸣

住址（医院）：黑龙江省伊春市乌翠区澜斌路 948 号彬智医院（邮政编码：842919）。联系电话：28568772。电子邮箱：juxhy@qxsymebp.health.cn

Zhù zhǐ: Sīkōng Nán Míng Hēilóngjiāng Shěng Yī Chūn Shì Wū Cuì Qū Lán Bīn Lù 948 Hào Bīn Zhì Yī Yuàn (Yóuzhèng Biānmǎ：842919). Liánxì Diànhuà：28568772. Diànzǐ Yóuxiāng：juxhy@qxsymebp.health.cn

Nan Ming Sikong, Bin Zhi Hospital, 948 Lan Bin Road, Wucui District, Yichun, Heilongjiang. Postal Code: 842919. Phone Number：28568772. E-mail：juxhy@qxsymebp.health.cn

704。姓名: 强土鸣

住址（公园）：黑龙江省佳木斯市桦川县学中路 560 号轶稼公园（邮政编码：804495）。联系电话：35252767。电子邮箱：sxvka@zocwabfq.parks.cn

Zhù zhǐ: Qiáng Tǔ Míng Hēilóngjiāng Shěng Jiāmùsī Shì Huà Chuān Xiàn Xué Zhōng Lù 560 Hào Yì Jià Gōng Yuán (Yóuzhèng Biānmǎ：804495). Liánxì Diànhuà：35252767. Diànzǐ Yóuxiāng：sxvka@zocwabfq.parks.cn

Tu Ming Qiang, Yi Jia Park, 560 Xue Zhong Road, Huachuan County, Jiamusi, Heilongjiang. Postal Code: 804495. Phone Number：35252767. E-mail：sxvka@zocwabfq.parks.cn

705。姓名: 蓟翼威

住址（机场）：黑龙江省大兴安岭地区新林区舟民路 929 号大兴安岭地区磊帆国际机场（邮政编码：131925）。联系电话：49578190。电子邮箱：vcnzm@zcuhgsdm.airports.cn

Zhù zhǐ: Jì Yì Wēi Hēilóngjiāng Shěng Dàxīngānlǐng Dìqū Xīn Lín Qū Zhōu Mín Lù 929 Hào Dàxīngānlǐng Dqū Lěi Fān Guó Jì Jī Chǎng (Yóuzhèng Biānmǎ：131925). Liánxì Diànhuà：49578190. Diànzǐ Yóuxiāng：vcnzm@zcuhgsdm.airports.cn

Yi Wei Ji, Da Hinggan Ling Lei Fan International Airport, 929 Zhou Min Road, Xinlin District, Da Hinggan Ling, Heilongjiang. Postal Code: 131925. Phone Number：49578190. E-mail：vcnzm@zcuhgsdm.airports.cn

706。姓名: 房可化

住址（大学）：黑龙江省鸡西市鸡东县辙际大学骥振路 444 号（邮政编码：709375）。联系电话：84414104。电子邮箱：uycft@pbtrdnmw.edu.cn

Zhù zhǐ: Fáng Kě Huà Hēilóngjiāng Shěng Jīxī Shì Jī Dōng Xiàn Zhé Jì DàxuéJì Zhèn Lù 444 Hào (Yóuzhèng Biānmǎ：709375). Liánxì Diànhuà：84414104. Diànzǐ Yóuxiāng：uycft@pbtrdnmw.edu.cn

Ke Hua Fang, Zhe Ji University, 444 Ji Zhen Road, Jidong County, Jixi, Heilongjiang. Postal Code: 709375. Phone Number：84414104. E-mail：uycft@pbtrdnmw.edu.cn

707。姓名: 印钊德

住址（家庭）：黑龙江省黑河市爱辉区王斌路 624 号淹黎公寓 13 层 533 室（邮政编码：720498）。联系电话：74731453。电子邮箱：luhne@aufbxlnm.cn

Zhù zhǐ: Yìn Zhāo Dé Hēilóngjiāng Shěng Hēihé Shì Ài Huī Qū Wáng Bīn Lù 624 Hào Yān Lí Gōng Yù 13 Céng 533 Shì (Yóuzhèng Biānmǎ：720498). Liánxì Diànhuà：74731453. Diànzǐ Yóuxiāng：luhne@aufbxlnm.cn

Zhao De Yin, Room# 533, Floor# 13, Yan Li Apartment, 624 Wang Bin Road, Aihui District, Heihe, Heilongjiang. Postal Code: 720498. Phone Number：74731453. E-mail：luhne@aufbxlnm.cn

708。姓名: 万进盛

住址（寺庙）：黑龙江省绥化市肇东市轼威路 367 号恩己寺（邮政编码：535519）。联系电话：65117585。电子邮箱：calkz@qugoljnm.god.cn

Zhù zhǐ: Wàn Jìn Chéng Hēilóngjiāng Shěng Suíhuà Shì Zhào Dōng Shì Shì Wēi Lù 367 Hào Ēn Jǐ Sì (Yóuzhèng Biānmǎ：535519). Liánxì Diànhuà：65117585. Diànzǐ Yóuxiāng：calkz@qugoljnm.god.cn

Jin Cheng Wan, En Ji Temple, 367 Shi Wei Road, Zhaodong, Suihua, Heilongjiang. Postal Code: 535519. Phone Number：65117585. E-mail：calkz@qugoljnm.god.cn

709。姓名: 贾冕食

住址（大学）：黑龙江省绥化市青冈县强其大学刚坡路 533 号（邮政编码：900289）。联系电话：70902009。电子邮箱：aczbr@hevikfcm.edu.cn

Zhù zhǐ: Jiǎ Miǎn Shí Hēilóngjiāng Shěng Suíhuà Shì Qīnggāng Xiàn Qiáng Qí DàxuéGāng Pō Lù 533 Hào（Yóuzhèng Biānmǎ：900289). Liánxì Diànhuà：70902009. Diànzǐ Yóuxiāng：aczbr@hevikfcm.edu.cn

Mian Shi Jia, Qiang Qi University, 533 Gang Po Road, Qinggang County, Suihua, Heilongjiang. Postal Code: 900289. Phone Number：70902009. E-mail：aczbr@hevikfcm.edu.cn

710。姓名: 容风院

住址（博物院）：黑龙江省牡丹江市绥芬河市国己路 288 号牡丹江博物馆（邮政编码：691662）。联系电话：18383776。电子邮箱：jvpmb@rwkounel.museums.cn

Zhù zhǐ: Róng Fēng Yuàn Hēilóngjiāng Shěng Mǔdānjiāng Shì Suífēnhé Shì Guó Jǐ Lù 288 Hào Mǔdānjiāng Bó Wù Guǎn（Yóuzhèng Biānmǎ：691662). Liánxì Diànhuà：18383776. Diànzǐ Yóuxiāng：jvpmb@rwkounel.museums.cn

Feng Yuan Rong, Mudanjiang Museum, 288 Guo Ji Road, Suifenhe, Mudanjiang, Heilongjiang. Postal Code: 691662. Phone Number：18383776. E-mail：jvpmb@rwkounel.museums.cn

711。姓名: 江进沛

住址（公共汽车站）：黑龙江省双鸭山市集贤县甫守路 258 号茂郁站（邮政编码：412261）。联系电话：56678022。电子邮箱：agkbm@zkfxujgc.transport.cn

Zhù zhǐ: Jiāng Jìn Bèi Hēilóngjiāng Shěng Shuāngyāshān Shì Jí Xián Xiàn Fǔ Shǒu Lù 258 Hào Mào Yù Zhàn（Yóuzhèng Biānmǎ：412261). Liánxì Diànhuà：56678022. Diànzǐ Yóuxiāng：agkbm@zkfxujgc.transport.cn

Jin Bei Jiang, Mao Yu Bus Station, 258 Fu Shou Road, Jixian County, Shuangyashan, Heilongjiang. Postal Code: 412261. Phone Number：56678022. E-mail：agkbm@zkfxujgc.transport.cn

712。姓名: 宗政汉石

住址（机场）：黑龙江省黑河市孙吴县鸣亚路 612 号黑河绅化国际机场（邮政编码：369349）。联系电话：44225815。电子邮箱：sjenf@rxiobask.airports.cn

Zhù zhǐ: Zōngzhèng Hàn Dàn Hēilóngjiāng Shěng Hēihé Shì Sūn Wúxiàn Míng Yà Lù 612 Hào Hēié Shēn Huà Guó Jì Jī Chǎng（Yóuzhèng Biānmǎ：369349). Liánxì Diànhuà：44225815. Diànzǐ Yóuxiāng：sjenf@rxiobask.airports.cn

Han Dan Zongzheng, Heihe Shen Hua International Airport, 612 Ming Ya Road, Sun Wu County, Heihe, Heilongjiang. Postal Code: 369349. Phone Number：44225815. E-mail：sjenf@rxiobask.airports.cn

713。姓名: 谯南智

住址（火车站）：黑龙江省齐齐哈尔市克山县振圣路 981 号齐齐哈尔站（邮政编码：361614）。联系电话：81745120。电子邮箱：irpfc@qsrydxfl.chr.cn

Zhù zhǐ: Qiáo Nán Zhì Hēilóngjiāng Shěng Qíqíhāěr Shì Kè Shān Xiàn Zhèn Shèng Lù 981 Hào Qíqíāěr Zhàn（Yóuzhèng Biānmǎ：361614). Liánxì Diànhuà：81745120. Diànzǐ Yóuxiāng：irpfc@qsrydxfl.chr.cn

Nan Zhi Qiao, Qiqihar Railway Station, 981 Zhen Sheng Road, Keshan County, Qiqihar, Heilongjiang. Postal Code: 361614. Phone Number：81745120. E-mail：irpfc@qsrydxfl.chr.cn

714。姓名: 郎全化

住址（公司）：黑龙江省佳木斯市同江市帆谢路 131 号维化有限公司（邮政编码：947601）。联系电话：98018118。电子邮箱：ajhyp@slrnbkao.biz.cn

Zhù zhǐ: Láng Quán Huā Hēilóngjiāng Shěng Jiāmùsī Shì Tóng Jiāng Shì Fān Xiè Lù 131 Hào Wéi Huà Yǒuxiàn Gōngsī（Yóuzhèng Biānmǎ：947601). Liánxì Diànhuà：98018118. Diànzǐ Yóuxiāng：ajhyp@slrnbkao.biz.cn

Quan Hua Lang, Wei Hua Corporation, 131 Fan Xie Road, Tongjiang City, Jiamusi, Heilongjiang. Postal Code: 947601. Phone Number：98018118. E-mail：ajhyp@slrnbkao.biz.cn

715。姓名: 秦可德

住址（博物院）：黑龙江省齐齐哈尔市克东县近冠路 360 号齐齐哈尔博物馆（邮政编码：559752）。联系电话：41444066。电子邮箱：bhexg@qdlymzko.museums.cn

Zhù zhǐ: Qín Kě Dé Hēilóngjiāng Shěng Qíqíhāěr Shì Kè Dōng Xiàn Jìn Guàn Lù 360 Hào Qíqíāěr Bó Wù Guǎn (Yóuzhèng Biānmǎ：559752). Liánxì Diànhuà：41444066. Diànzǐ Yóuxiāng：bhexg@qdlymzko.museums.cn

Ke De Qin, Qiqihar Museum, 360 Jin Guan Road, Kedong County, Qiqihar, Heilongjiang. Postal Code: 559752. Phone Number：41444066. E-mail：bhexg@qdlymzko.museums.cn

716。姓名: 包磊懂

住址（大学）：黑龙江省黑河市五大连池市铁亮大学国食路 904 号（邮政编码：487423）。联系电话：75175375。电子邮箱：cqwyr@menqwpyo.edu.cn

Zhù zhǐ: Bāo Lěi Dǒng Hēilóngjiāng Shěng Hēihé Shì Wǔdàliánchí Shì Fū Liàng DàxuéGuó Sì Lù 904 Hào (Yóuzhèng Biānmǎ：487423). Liánxì Diànhuà：75175375. Diànzǐ Yóuxiāng：cqwyr@menqwpyo.edu.cn

Lei Dong Bao, Fu Liang University, 904 Guo Si Road, Wudalianchi City, Heihe, Heilongjiang. Postal Code: 487423. Phone Number：75175375. E-mail：cqwyr@menqwpyo.edu.cn

717。姓名: 柏石尚

住址（寺庙）：黑龙江省绥化市青冈县王独路 338 号钦鸣寺（邮政编码：166294）。联系电话：56939974。电子邮箱：dfbvc@dknjgflz.god.cn

Zhù zhǐ: Bǎi Dàn Shàng Hēilóngjiāng Shěng Suíhuà Shì Qīnggāng Xiàn Wáng Dú Lù 338 Hào Qīn Míng Sì (Yóuzhèng Biānmǎ：166294). Liánxì Diànhuà：56939974. Diànzǐ Yóuxiāng：dfbvc@dknjgflz.god.cn

Dan Shang Bai, Qin Ming Temple, 338 Wang Du Road, Qinggang County, Suihua, Heilongjiang. Postal Code: 166294. Phone Number：56939974. E-mail：dfbvc@dknjgflz.god.cn

718。姓名: 单于亮焯

住址（机场）：黑龙江省鸡西市麻山区翰金路 946 号鸡西庆骥国际机场（邮政编码：367954）。联系电话：14127571。电子邮箱：woctu@kqixvlpo.airports.cn

Zhù zhǐ: Chányú Liàng Chāo Hēilóngjiāng Shěng Jīxī Shì Má Shānqū Hàn Jīn Lù 946 Hào Jīxī Qìng Jì Guó Jì Jī Chǎng (Yóuzhèng Biānmǎ：367954). Liánxì Diànhuà：14127571. Diànzǐ Yóuxiāng：woctu@kqixvlpo.airports.cn

Liang Chao Chanyu, Jixi Qing Ji International Airport, 946 Han Jin Road, Mashan District, Jixi, Heilongjiang. Postal Code: 367954. Phone Number：14127571. E-mail：woctu@kqixvlpo.airports.cn

719。姓名: 卞易洵

住址（公司）：黑龙江省牡丹江市林口县独先路 332 号科祥有限公司（邮政编码：252463）。联系电话：34292931。电子邮箱：jlgvq@lxtajzyg.biz.cn

Zhù zhǐ: Biàn Yì Xún Hēilóngjiāng Shěng Mǔdānjiāng Shì Línkǒu Xiàn Dú Xiān Lù 332 Hào Kē Xiáng Yǒuxiàn Gōngsī (Yóuzhèng Biānmǎ：252463). Liánxì Diànhuà：34292931. Diànzǐ Yóuxiāng：jlgvq@lxtajzyg.biz.cn

Yi Xun Bian, Ke Xiang Corporation, 332 Du Xian Road, Linkou County, Mudanjiang, Heilongjiang. Postal Code: 252463. Phone Number：34292931. E-mail：jlgvq@lxtajzyg.biz.cn

720。姓名: 慕进鹤

住址（医院）：黑龙江省鸡西市麻山区食宝路 929 号易宝医院（邮政编码：728755）。联系电话：47021921。电子邮箱：gblet@osixgzhq.health.cn

Zhù zhǐ: Mù Jìn Hè Hēilóngjiāng Shěng Jīxī Shì Má Shānqū Yì Bǎo Lù 929 Hào Yì Bǎo Yī Yuàn (Yóuzhèng Biānmǎ：728755). Liánxì Diànhuà：47021921. Diànzǐ Yóuxiāng：gblet@osixgzhq.health.cn

Jin He Mu, Yi Bao Hospital, 929 Yi Bao Road, Mashan District, Jixi, Heilongjiang. Postal Code: 728755. Phone Number：47021921. E-mail：gblet@osixgzhq.health.cn

CHAPTER 5: NAMES & LOCATIONS (121-150)

721。姓名: 匡近敬

住址（医院）：黑龙江省伊春市汤旺县队楚路 148 号食顺医院（邮政编码：852124）。联系电话：16373096。电子邮箱：objid@tzhjuybe.health.cn

Zhù zhǐ: Kuāng Jìn Jìng Hēilóngjiāng Shěng Yī Chūn Shì Tāng Wàng Xiàn Duì Chǔ Lù 148 Hào Yì Shùn Yī Yuàn (Yóuzhèng Biānmǎ：852124). Liánxì Diànhuà：16373096. Diànzǐ Yóuxiāng：objid@tzhjuybe.health.cn

Jin Jing Kuang, Yi Shun Hospital, 148 Dui Chu Road, Tangwang County, Yichun, Heilongjiang. Postal Code: 852124. Phone Number：16373096. E-mail：objid@tzhjuybe.health.cn

722。姓名: 有绅坡

住址（湖泊）：黑龙江省大兴安岭地区松岭区乙顺路 258 号宝轶湖（邮政编码：132316）。联系电话：12602291。电子邮箱：hjqly@cfdglsjy.lakes.cn

Zhù zhǐ: Yǒu Shēn Pō Hēilóngjiāng Shěng Dàxīngānlǐng Dìqū Sōng Lǐng Qū Yǐ Shùn Lù 258 Hào Bǎo Yì Hú (Yóuzhèng Biānmǎ：132316). Liánxì Diànhuà：12602291. Diànzǐ Yóuxiāng：hjqly@cfdglsjy.lakes.cn

Shen Po You, Bao Yi Lake, 258 Yi Shun Road, Songling District, Da Hinggan Ling, Heilongjiang. Postal Code: 132316. Phone Number：12602291. E-mail：hjqly@cfdglsjy.lakes.cn

723。姓名: 顾风舟

住址（家庭）：黑龙江省黑河市孙吴县乙鹤路 833 号亮院公寓 20 层 190 室（邮政编码：595741）。联系电话：19897720。电子邮箱：fmzqr@qzignhfa.cn

Zhù zhǐ: Gù Fēng Zhōu Hēilóngjiāng Shěng Hēihé Shì Sūn Wúxiàn Yǐ Hè Lù 833 Hào Liàng Yuàn Gōng Yù 20 Céng 190 Shì (Yóuzhèng Biānmǎ：595741). Liánxì Diànhuà：19897720. Diànzǐ Yóuxiāng：fmzqr@qzignhfa.cn

Feng Zhou Gu, Room# 190, Floor# 20, Liang Yuan Apartment, 833 Yi He Road, Sun Wu County, Heihe, Heilongjiang. Postal Code: 595741. Phone Number：19897720. E-mail：fmzqr@qzignhfa.cn

724。姓名: 慕容金石

住址（公司）：黑龙江省佳木斯市东风区学勇路 243 号圣屹有限公司（邮政编码：229127）。联系电话：75782760。电子邮箱：sdxbu@gxzsvcbl.biz.cn

Zhù zhǐ: Mùróng Jīn Shí Hēilóngjiāng Shěng Jiāmùsī Shì Dōngfēng Qū Xué Yǒng Lù 243 Hào Shèng Yì Yǒuxiàn Gōngsī (Yóuzhèng Biānmǎ：229127). Liánxì Diànhuà：75782760. Diànzǐ Yóuxiāng：sdxbu@gxzsvcbl.biz.cn

Jin Shi Murong, Sheng Yi Corporation, 243 Xue Yong Road, Dongfeng District, Jiamusi, Heilongjiang. Postal Code: 229127. Phone Number：75782760. E-mail：sdxbu@gxzsvcbl.biz.cn

725。姓名: 郭舟可

住址（广场）：黑龙江省大兴安岭地区新林区中辙路 765 号光奎广场（邮政编码：384550）。联系电话：27379558。电子邮箱：bglrq@hjkgieap.squares.cn

Zhù zhǐ: Guō Zhōu Kě Hēilóngjiāng Shěng Dàxīngānlǐng Dìqū Xīn Lín Qū Zhòng Zhé Lù 765 Hào Guāng Kuí Guǎng Chǎng (Yóuzhèng Biānmǎ：384550). Liánxì Diànhuà：27379558. Diànzǐ Yóuxiāng：bglrq@hjkgieap.squares.cn

Zhou Ke Guo, Guang Kui Square, 765 Zhong Zhe Road, Xinlin District, Da Hinggan Ling, Heilongjiang. Postal Code: 384550. Phone Number：27379558. E-mail：bglrq@hjkgieap.squares.cn

726。姓名: 许恩阳

住址（公共汽车站）：黑龙江省七台河市茄子河区茂坤路 286 号不德站（邮政编码：484584）。联系电话：50074653。电子邮箱：fvxdn@mpjarieq.transport.cn

Zhù zhǐ: Xǔ Ēn Yáng Hēilóngjiāng Shěng Qī Tái Hé Shì Qiézi Hé Qū Mào Kūn Lù 286 Hào Bù Dé Zhàn (Yóuzhèng Biānmǎ：484584). Liánxì Diànhuà：50074653. Diànzǐ Yóuxiāng：fvxdn@mpjarieq.transport.cn

En Yang Xu, Bu De Bus Station, 286 Mao Kun Road, Eggplant River District, Qitaihe, Heilongjiang. Postal Code: 484584. Phone Number：50074653. E-mail：fvxdn@mpjarieq.transport.cn

727。姓名: 魏钊渊

住址（寺庙）：黑龙江省七台河市桃山区刚澜路 320 号乐员寺（邮政编码：122206）。联系电话：64686383。电子邮箱：rtqhp@dwulstvf.god.cn

Zhù zhǐ: Wèi Zhāo Yuān Hēilóngjiāng Shěng Qī Tái Hé Shì Táoshānqū Gāng Lán Lù 320 Hào Lè Yún Sì（Yóuzhèng Biānmǎ：122206). Liánxì Diànhuà：64686383. Diànzǐ Yóuxiāng：rtqhp@dwulstvf.god.cn

Zhao Yuan Wei, Le Yun Temple, 320 Gang Lan Road, Taoshan District, Qitaihe, Heilongjiang. Postal Code: 122206. Phone Number：64686383. E-mail：rtqhp@dwulstvf.god.cn

728。姓名: 吕仲腾

住址（公司）：黑龙江省伊春市伊美区九翼路 842 号星可有限公司（邮政编码：163017）。联系电话：95929299。电子邮箱：ronpa@gahqrpmz.biz.cn

Zhù zhǐ: Lǚ Zhòng Téng Hēilóngjiāng Shěng Yī Chūn Shì Yīměi Qū Jiǔ Yì Lù 842 Hào Xīng Kě Yǒuxiàn Gōngsī（Yóuzhèng Biānmǎ：163017). Liánxì Diànhuà：95929299. Diànzǐ Yóuxiāng：ronpa@gahqrpmz.biz.cn

Zhong Teng Llv, Xing Ke Corporation, 842 Jiu Yi Road, Immi District, Yichun, Heilongjiang. Postal Code: 163017. Phone Number：95929299. E-mail：ronpa@gahqrpmz.biz.cn

729。姓名: 贡亮陶

住址（医院）：黑龙江省大兴安岭地区呼玛县谢稼路 164 号乐愈医院（邮政编码：854964）。联系电话：25863182。电子邮箱：fcuvq@ktrfoqnd.health.cn

Zhù zhǐ: Gòng Liàng Táo Hēilóngjiāng Shěng Dàxīngānlǐng Dìqū Hū Mǎ Xiàn Xiè Jià Lù 164 Hào Lè Yù Yī Yuàn（Yóuzhèng Biānmǎ：854964). Liánxì Diànhuà：25863182. Diànzǐ Yóuxiāng：fcuvq@ktrfoqnd.health.cn

Liang Tao Gong, Le Yu Hospital, 164 Xie Jia Road, Huma County, Da Hinggan Ling, Heilongjiang. Postal Code: 854964. Phone Number：25863182. E-mail：fcuvq@ktrfoqnd.health.cn

730。姓名: 年白智

住址（火车站）：黑龙江省鸡西市恒山区顺九路 121 号鸡西站（邮政编码：437096）。联系电话：92482028。电子邮箱：pnstj@ixpuzrch.chr.cn

Zhù zhǐ: Nián Bái Zhì Hēilóngjiāng Shěng Jīxī Shì Héngshānqū Shùn Jiǔ Lù 121 Hào Jīxī Zhàn（Yóuzhèng Biānmǎ：437096）. Liánxì Diànhuà：92482028. Diànzǐ Yóuxiāng：pnstj@ixpuzrch.chr.cn

Bai Zhi Nian, Jixi Railway Station, 121 Shun Jiu Road, Hengshan District, Jixi, Heilongjiang. Postal Code: 437096. Phone Number：92482028. E-mail：pnstj@ixpuzrch.chr.cn

731。姓名: 窦德福

住址（家庭）：黑龙江省绥化市庆安县进启路 834 号翰沛公寓 48 层 194 室（邮政编码：848438）。联系电话：71747590。电子邮箱：lybnv@arymucgi.cn

Zhù zhǐ: Dòu Dé Fú Hēilóngjiāng Shěng Suíhuà Shì Qìng Ān Xiàn Jìn Qǐ Lù 834 Hào Hàn Bèi Gōng Yù 48 Céng 194 Shì (Yóuzhèng Biānmǎ：848438). Liánxì Diànhuà：71747590. Diànzǐ Yóuxiāng：lybnv@arymucgi.cn

De Fu Dou, Room# 194, Floor# 48, Han Bei Apartment, 834 Jin Qi Road, Qingan County, Suihua, Heilongjiang. Postal Code: 848438. Phone Number：71747590. E-mail：lybnv@arymucgi.cn

732。姓名: 戚启人

住址（酒店）：黑龙江省哈尔滨市通河县磊中路 270 号焯柱酒店（邮政编码：198109）。联系电话：51119122。电子邮箱：lfwtv@ynplhaju.biz.cn

Zhù zhǐ: Qī Qǐ Rén Hēilóngjiāng Shěng Hāěrbīn Shì Tōng Hé Xiàn Lěi Zhōng Lù 270 Hào Chāo Zhù Jiǔ Diàn（Yóuzhèng Biānmǎ：198109）. Liánxì Diànhuà：51119122. Diànzǐ Yóuxiāng：lfwtv@ynplhaju.biz.cn

Qi Ren Qi, Chao Zhu Hotel, 270 Lei Zhong Road, Tonghe County, Harbin, Heilongjiang. Postal Code: 198109. Phone Number：51119122. E-mail：lfwtv@ynplhaju.biz.cn

733。姓名: 黎腾克

住址（机场）：黑龙江省七台河市勃利县学陆路 786 号七台河际毅国际机场（邮政编码：271749）。联系电话：26566852。电子邮箱：ygfvt@zducxlnw.airports.cn

Zhù zhǐ: Lí Téng Kè Hēilóngjiāng Shěng Qī Tái Hé Shì Bó Lì Xiàn Xué Lù Lù 786 Hào Qī Tái Hé Jì Yì Guó Jì Jī Chǎng (Yóuzhèng Biānmǎ：271749). Liánxì Diànhuà：26566852. Diànzǐ Yóuxiāng：ygfvt@zducxlnw.airports.cn

Teng Ke Li, Qitaihe Ji Yi International Airport, 786 Xue Lu Road, Burleigh County, Qitaihe, Heilongjiang. Postal Code: 271749. Phone Number：26566852. E-mail：ygfvt@zducxlnw.airports.cn

734。姓名: 索沛绅

住址（湖泊）：黑龙江省黑河市逊克县澜仓路 154 号禹食湖（邮政编码：395044）。联系电话：33046663。电子邮箱：ikfrz@btfrpayl.lakes.cn

Zhù zhǐ: Suǒ Pèi Shēn Hēilóngjiāng Shěng Hēihé Shì Xùn Kè Xiàn Lán Cāng Lù 154 Hào Yǔ Sì Hú (Yóuzhèng Biānmǎ：395044). Liánxì Diànhuà：33046663. Diànzǐ Yóuxiāng：ikfrz@btfrpayl.lakes.cn

Pei Shen Suo, Yu Si Lake, 154 Lan Cang Road, Sunk County, Heihe, Heilongjiang. Postal Code: 395044. Phone Number：33046663. E-mail：ikfrz@btfrpayl.lakes.cn

735。姓名: 阮强舟

住址（医院）：黑龙江省齐齐哈尔市克东县甫舟路 866 号陆学医院（邮政编码：190404）。联系电话：66253199。电子邮箱：mfrsa@tmoxbqrj.health.cn

Zhù zhǐ: Ruǎn Qiǎng Zhōu Hēilóngjiāng Shěng Qíqíhāěr Shì Kè Dōng Xiàn Fǔ Zhōu Lù 866 Hào Lù Xué Yī Yuàn (Yóuzhèng Biānmǎ：190404). Liánxì Diànhuà：66253199. Diànzǐ Yóuxiāng：mfrsa@tmoxbqrj.health.cn

Qiang Zhou Ruan, Lu Xue Hospital, 866 Fu Zhou Road, Kedong County, Qiqihar, Heilongjiang. Postal Code: 190404. Phone Number：66253199. E-mail：mfrsa@tmoxbqrj.health.cn

736。姓名: 容斌懂

住址（博物院）：黑龙江省牡丹江市东安区继汉路 430 号牡丹江博物馆（邮政编码：950682）。联系电话：23626212。电子邮箱：orkyl@krlwngtc.museums.cn

Zhù zhǐ: Róng Bīn Dǒng Hēilóngjiāng Shěng Mǔdānjiāng Shì Dōngān Qū Jì Hàn Lù 430 Hào Mǔdānjiāng Bó Wù Guǎn（Yóuzhèng Biānmǎ：950682). Liánxì Diànhuà：23626212. Diànzǐ Yóuxiāng：orkyl@krlwngtc.museums.cn

Bin Dong Rong, Mudanjiang Museum, 430 Ji Han Road, Dongan District, Mudanjiang, Heilongjiang. Postal Code: 950682. Phone Number：23626212. E-mail：orkyl@krlwngtc.museums.cn

737。姓名: 任土超

住址（广场）：黑龙江省哈尔滨市南岗区俊振路 177 号豪福广场（邮政编码：631578）。联系电话：57481654。电子邮箱：avimc@kzigxmbw.squares.cn

Zhù zhǐ: Rèn Tǔ Chāo Hēilóngjiāng Shěng Hāěrbīn Shì Nángǎng Qū Jùn Zhèn Lù 177 Hào Háo Fú Guǎng Chǎng（Yóuzhèng Biānmǎ：631578). Liánxì Diànhuà：57481654. Diànzǐ Yóuxiāng：avimc@kzigxmbw.squares.cn

Tu Chao Ren, Hao Fu Square, 177 Jun Zhen Road, Nangang District, Harbin, Heilongjiang. Postal Code: 631578. Phone Number：57481654. E-mail：avimc@kzigxmbw.squares.cn

738。姓名: 利寰智

住址（公园）：黑龙江省鹤岗市工农区熔员路 223 号员恩公园（邮政编码：813834）。联系电话：95940363。电子邮箱：hekul@dcgrnkbf.parks.cn

Zhù zhǐ: Lì Huán Zhì Hēilóngjiāng Shěng Hè Gǎng Shì Gōngnóng Qū Róng Yuán Lù 223 Hào Yún Ēn Gōng Yuán（Yóuzhèng Biānmǎ：813834). Liánxì Diànhuà：95940363. Diànzǐ Yóuxiāng：hekul@dcgrnkbf.parks.cn

Huan Zhi Li, Yun En Park, 223 Rong Yuan Road, Industrial And Agricultural Area, Hegang, Heilongjiang. Postal Code: 813834. Phone Number：95940363. E-mail：hekul@dcgrnkbf.parks.cn

739。姓名: 何澜屹

住址（寺庙）：黑龙江省七台河市勃利县山俊路 156 号谢茂寺（邮政编码：178877）。联系电话：11756920。电子邮箱：ryxcg@mbgrxqel.god.cn

Zhù zhǐ: Hé Lán Yì Hēilóngjiāng Shěng Qī Tái Hé Shì Bó Lì Xiàn Shān Jùn Lù 156 Hào Xiè Mào Sì (Yóuzhèng Biānmǎ：178877). Liánxì Diànhuà：11756920. Diànzǐ Yóuxiāng：ryxcg@mbgrxqel.god.cn

Lan Yi He, Xie Mao Temple, 156 Shan Jun Road, Burleigh County, Qitaihe, Heilongjiang. Postal Code: 178877. Phone Number：11756920. E-mail：ryxcg@mbgrxqel.god.cn

740。姓名: 廉民继

住址（湖泊）：黑龙江省大兴安岭地区加格达奇区大维路 521 号易翰湖（邮政编码：619807）。联系电话：75758317。电子邮箱：groha@euibcmgh.lakes.cn

Zhù zhǐ: Lián Mín Jì Hēilóngjiāng Shěng Dàxīngānlǐng Dìqū Jiā Gé Dá Qí Qū Dài Wéi Lù 521 Hào Yì Hàn Hú (Yóuzhèng Biānmǎ：619807). Liánxì Diànhuà：75758317. Diànzǐ Yóuxiāng：groha@euibcmgh.lakes.cn

Min Ji Lian, Yi Han Lake, 521 Dai Wei Road, Gagedaqi District, Da Hinggan Ling, Heilongjiang. Postal Code: 619807. Phone Number：75758317. E-mail：groha@euibcmgh.lakes.cn

741。姓名: 司寇水科

住址（家庭）：黑龙江省齐齐哈尔市甘南县豪岐路 374 号亚豪公寓 3 层 534 室（邮政编码：322846）。联系电话：21254170。电子邮箱：qnbst@ohfsgwpl.cn

Zhù zhǐ: Sīkòu Shuǐ Kē Hēilóngjiāng Shěng Qíqíhāěr Shì Gānnán Xiàn Háo Qí Lù 374 Hào Yà Háo Gōng Yù 3 Céng 534 Shì (Yóuzhèng Biānmǎ：322846). Liánxì Diànhuà：21254170. Diànzǐ Yóuxiāng：qnbst@ohfsgwpl.cn

Shui Ke Sikou, Room# 534, Floor# 3, Ya Hao Apartment, 374 Hao Qi Road, Gannan County, Qiqihar, Heilongjiang. Postal Code: 322846. Phone Number：21254170. E-mail：qnbst@ohfsgwpl.cn

742。姓名: 唐食柱

住址（医院）: 黑龙江省大庆市红岗区屹桥路 428 号食甫医院（邮政编码：867724）。联系电话：47673510。电子邮箱：vzhlc@yrfkhwvc.health.cn

Zhù zhǐ: Táng Yì Zhù Hēilóngjiāng Shěng Dàqìng Shì Hónggǎng Qū Yì Qiáo Lù 428 Hào Yì Fǔ Yī Yuàn (Yóuzhèng Biānmǎ：867724). Liánxì Diànhuà：47673510. Diànzǐ Yóuxiāng：vzhlc@yrfkhwvc.health.cn

Yi Zhu Tang, Yi Fu Hospital, 428 Yi Qiao Road, Honggang District, Daqing, Heilongjiang. Postal Code: 867724. Phone Number：47673510. E-mail：vzhlc@yrfkhwvc.health.cn

743。姓名: 贝风全

住址（公共汽车站）: 黑龙江省哈尔滨市尚志市桥发路 869 号发豹站（邮政编码：350283）。联系电话：18877130。电子邮箱：ehdyq@imuhfbnw.transport.cn

Zhù zhǐ: Bèi Fēng Quán Hēilóngjiāng Shěng Hāěrbīn Shì Shàngzhì Shì Qiáo Fā Lù 869 Hào Fā Bào Zhàn (Yóuzhèng Biānmǎ：350283). Liánxì Diànhuà：18877130. Diànzǐ Yóuxiāng：ehdyq@imuhfbnw.transport.cn

Feng Quan Bei, Fa Bao Bus Station, 869 Qiao Fa Road, Shangzhi City, Harbin, Heilongjiang. Postal Code: 350283. Phone Number：18877130. E-mail：ehdyq@imuhfbnw.transport.cn

744。姓名: 宗懂惟

住址（酒店）: 黑龙江省牡丹江市阳明区桥跃路 808 号渊迅酒店（邮政编码：479709）。联系电话：48085442。电子邮箱：smbgq@clfdqgyb.biz.cn

Zhù zhǐ: Zōng Dǒng Wéi Hēilóngjiāng Shěng Mǔdānjiāng Shì Yáng Míng Qū Qiáo Yuè Lù 808 Hào Yuān Xùn Jiǔ Diàn (Yóuzhèng Biānmǎ：479709). Liánxì Diànhuà：48085442. Diànzǐ Yóuxiāng：smbgq@clfdqgyb.biz.cn

Dong Wei Zong, Yuan Xun Hotel, 808 Qiao Yue Road, Yangming District, Mudanjiang, Heilongjiang. Postal Code: 479709. Phone Number：48085442. E-mail：smbgq@clfdqgyb.biz.cn

745。姓名: 鲜于智浩

住址（湖泊）：黑龙江省七台河市茄子河区歧臻路 957 号员胜湖（邮政编码：385713）。联系电话：19728585。电子邮箱：mrtgw@nletqbyv.lakes.cn

Zhù zhǐ: Xiānyú Zhì Hào Hēilóngjiāng Shěng Qī Tái Hé Shì Qiézi Hé Qū Qí Zhēn Lù 957 Hào Yún Shēng Hú (Yóuzhèng Biānmǎ：385713). Liánxì Diànhuà：19728585. Diànzǐ Yóuxiāng：mrtgw@nletqbyv.lakes.cn

Zhi Hao Xianyu, Yun Sheng Lake, 957 Qi Zhen Road, Eggplant River District, Qitaihe, Heilongjiang. Postal Code: 385713. Phone Number：19728585. E-mail：mrtgw@nletqbyv.lakes.cn

746。姓名: 松圣院

住址（广场）：黑龙江省七台河市茄子河区世振路 792 号涛翼广场（邮政编码：686927）。联系电话：46425961。电子邮箱：ahced@edyjgxlr.squares.cn

Zhù zhǐ: Sōng Shèng Yuàn Hēilóngjiāng Shěng Qī Tái Hé Shì Qiézi Hé Qū Shì Zhèn Lù 792 Hào Tāo Yì Guǎng Chǎng (Yóuzhèng Biānmǎ：686927). Liánxì Diànhuà：46425961. Diànzǐ Yóuxiāng：ahced@edyjgxlr.squares.cn

Sheng Yuan Song, Tao Yi Square, 792 Shi Zhen Road, Eggplant River District, Qitaihe, Heilongjiang. Postal Code: 686927. Phone Number：46425961. E-mail：ahced@edyjgxlr.squares.cn

747。姓名: 武敬毅

住址（公共汽车站）：黑龙江省牡丹江市东安区自南路 633 号石桥站（邮政编码：273796）。联系电话：76440288。电子邮箱：iekwr@qsdptjxh.transport.cn

Zhù zhǐ: Wǔ Jìng Yì Hēilóngjiāng Shěng Mǔdānjiāng Shì Dōngān Qū Zì Nán Lù 633 Hào Shí Qiáo Zhàn (Yóuzhèng Biānmǎ：273796). Liánxì Diànhuà：76440288. Diànzǐ Yóuxiāng：iekwr@qsdptjxh.transport.cn

Jing Yi Wu, Shi Qiao Bus Station, 633 Zi Nan Road, Dongan District, Mudanjiang, Heilongjiang. Postal Code: 273796. Phone Number：76440288. E-mail：iekwr@qsdptjxh.transport.cn

748。姓名: 嵇汉俊

住址（寺庙）：黑龙江省双鸭山市四方台区俊沛路 395 号红宝寺（邮政编码：167111）。联系电话：58366840。电子邮箱：foxqv@zaldspyj.god.cn

Zhù zhǐ: Jī Hàn Jùn Hēilóngjiāng Shěng Shuāngyāshān Shì Sìfāng Tái Qū Jùn Bèi Lù 395 Hào Hóng Bǎo Sì（Yóuzhèng Biānmǎ：167111). Liánxì Diànhuà：58366840. Diànzǐ Yóuxiāng：foxqv@zaldspyj.god.cn

Han Jun Ji, Hong Bao Temple, 395 Jun Bei Road, Sifangtai District, Shuangyashan, Heilongjiang. Postal Code: 167111. Phone Number：58366840. E-mail：foxqv@zaldspyj.god.cn

749。姓名: 亓官院刚

住址（公司）：黑龙江省佳木斯市郊区中歧路 240 号波恩有限公司（邮政编码：422248）。联系电话：71280496。电子邮箱：iqjuv@yiodakjp.biz.cn

Zhù zhǐ: Qíguān Yuàn Gāng Hēilóngjiāng Shěng Jiāmùsī Shì Jiāoqū Zhōng Qí Lù 240 Hào Bō Ēn Yǒuxiàn Gōngsī（Yóuzhèng Biānmǎ：422248). Liánxì Diànhuà：71280496. Diànzǐ Yóuxiāng：iqjuv@yiodakjp.biz.cn

Yuan Gang Qiguan, Bo En Corporation, 240 Zhong Qi Road, Jiao District, Jiamusi, Heilongjiang. Postal Code: 422248. Phone Number：71280496. E-mail：iqjuv@yiodakjp.biz.cn

750。姓名: 蔺石谢

住址（机场）：黑龙江省大兴安岭地区新林区焯院路 382 号大兴安岭地区强领国际机场（邮政编码：287809）。联系电话：94863130。电子邮箱：tquhd@opicnkhd.airports.cn

Zhù zhǐ: Lìn Shí Xiè Hēilóngjiāng Shěng Dàxīngānlǐng Dìqū Xīn Lín Qū Zhuō Yuàn Lù 382 Hào Dàxīngānlǐng Dqū Qiǎng Lǐng Guó Jì Jī Chǎng (Yóuzhèng Biānmǎ: 287809). Liánxì Diànhuà: 94863130. Diànzǐ Yóuxiāng: tquhd@opicnkhd.airports.cn

Shi Xie Lin, Da Hinggan Ling Qiang Ling International Airport, 382 Zhuo Yuan Road, Xinlin District, Da Hinggan Ling, Heilongjiang. Postal Code: 287809. Phone Number: 94863130. E-mail: tquhd@opicnkhd.airports.cn

Milton Keynes UK
Ingram Content Group UK Ltd.
UKHW020819141024
449536UK00011B/111

9 798887 348407